Partners in Covenant

Partners in Covenant
The Art of Spiritual Companionship

Barbara A. Sheehan, S.P.

The Pilgrim Press
Cleveland, Ohio

To Ken, Julie, Terry, and M. Joan,

who have been dedicated spiritual guides in my life

The Pilgrim Press, Cleveland, Ohio 44115
© 1999 by Barbara A. Sheehan, S.P.

Altered from *Pastoral Counseling across Cultures,* by David W. Augsburger. © 1986 David Augsburger. Used by permission of Westminster John Knox Press. • Focusing exercise adapted from Peter A. Campbell and Edwin M. McMahon, *Bio-Spirituality: Focusing as a Way to Grow* (Chicago: Loyola Press, 1985). Used by permission.

Biblical quotations are from the New Revised Standard Version of the Bible, © 1989 by the Division of Christian Education of the National Council of the Churches of Christ in the U.S.A., and are used by permission. Adaptations have been made for inclusivity.

04   03   02   01   00   99   5   4   3   2   1

Library of Congress Cataloging-in-Publication Data

Sheehan, Barbara A. (Barbara Ann), 1942–
    Partners in covenant : the art of spiritual companionship /
Barbara A. Sheehan.
        p.   cm.
    Includes bibliographical references and index.
    ISBN 0-8298-1329-2 (pbk. : alk. paper)
    1. Spiritual formation.   2. Fellowship—Religious aspects—Christianity.   I. Title.
BV4517.5.S54   1999
248.4—dc21   98-50598
                                                                                  CIP

Contents

Preface

The Christian community is a community of care. Christians profess to care for all of creation and for all creatures. Their care focuses on building the reign of God in the here and now of human reality. Their care touches the whole community as members exercise their particular gifts among and for the community. Some are gifted as ordained care providers, and others are gifted as lay caregivers. Some are gifted to be prophets, teachers, pastors, or leaders in other ways. Many members of the Christian community (ordained and nonordained) are called to express and share their gifts in the ministry of spirituality. They are called to companion their brothers and sisters along the path of spiritual growth.

Spiritual companions are persons of faith willing to enter into a helping relationship with others on their spiritual journey. Companions are not teachers or persons who have answers but partners who take seriously the concerns and experiences of those with whom they journey. Spiritual companions share in the lives of others through attentive listening, empathic responding, and caring reflection on what they have heard in the lived experiences of their peer(s). Within this partnership, a modern-day Emmaus journey, spiritual companions join with others of faith in their ongoing process of discovering and responding to the Divine Presence in human reality.

Spiritual companionship is a ministry and an art much needed today among Christians. People yearn for meaning and for a life of spiritual connection with their experiences in an often disconnected and seemingly meaningless world.

There are compassionate Christians, themselves growing spiritually, desirous of walking with their sisters and brothers in discovering meaning and connection with the Divine. Yet they lack the skills and knowledge that enable them to commit to the ministry of spiritual companionship within the Christian community. They need nurturance and guidance to become competent and faithful artisans on this spiritual walk.

Partners in Covenant is informative and formative. It offers practical instructional material integrated with concrete examples and reflection for one's personal formation and development. It also provides the framework for a comprehensive program of training that can revitalize the spiritual caring ministry of Christian communities.

This book is for persons wishing to become faithful stewards of their call and gifts as effective spiritual companions within the Christian community. Thus, this book is for individuals, congregation-based groups, seminary colloquium and staff groups, clergy, religious women and men, Christian formation guides and personnel, chaplains and hospice teams, small Christian communities, presbytery and ordination bodies, congregational staffs, and faith-sharing groups. It is for those beginning the ministry of spiritual companionship and for those desirous of renewal and updating as spiritual companions.

Essential to the ministry of Christian spirituality is peership. The ministry of spiritual companionship is not a hierarchical ministry (relegated solely to clergypersons) but a ministry of peers who covenant, as God covenants with them, to be in companioning relationship with one another. The Christian community (a microcosm of the world) is also diversified in cultural heritage, ethnicity, personality formation, gender expression, and spiritual needs and expressions.

A conviction of this book is that effective spiritual companioning, besides being a peer ministry, is a contextual ministry of care; it attends to the context and unique experiences in the personal and communal lives of those being companioned. The familial and societal context and experiences of persons impact their spiritual journey.

Partners in Covenant, then, is a reflective guide for the personal formation and spiritual maturation of persons wishing to become more effective spiritual companions. It offers instructional material, concrete experiential examples, and reflection tools for the Christian companion to become more knowledgeable, to gain practical skills, and to grow personally as a spiritual companion. Throughout this book I have given direct guidance in the use of prayer forms as a spiritual companion, and I have provided the format and structure for persons to learn the art of spiritual companionship as Christian peers within a community context.

Chapter 1 sets the stage for the person called to the ministry of spiritual companionship. It focuses on the call to the ministry of spiritual companionship; on the nature, context, and art of listening; and on the qualities of persons called to this ministry. Chapter 2 guides the reader toward a theological and biblical grounding from which to companion another. Chapter 3 explains and illustrates the seven basic elements of effective listening and identifies major pitfalls for the companion to avoid. It is a key chapter in helping the companion to become an effective listener.

Chapters 4 and 5 discuss prayer and images of God as related to spiritual development. These chapters open up new possibilities of prayer forms and images for the companion both in one's ministry and in one's relationship with God. (Nine specific forms of prayer are described in Appendix A because many exercises at the ends of chapters make reference to them.) Chapter 5 connects the common themes of the Judeo-Christian heritage with today's spiritual journeyer. These chapters guide the companion to reflect on the diversity of prayer and images of God, to affirm one's own style of prayer and images, and to become open to being transformed spiritually.

Chapter 6 discusses personality theories and authority in light of cultural, ethnic, and gender differences as related to spiritual companioning. In addition it gives an understanding of the Myers-Briggs Type Indicator and the Enneagram typology that helps the companion develop competency in being open to the uniqueness of the Christian journeyer. Chapter 7 grounds the companion in the richness of the Judeo-Christian spiritual tradition, connects the psychological understandings of chapter 6 with spiritual development, and discusses the spirituality of white males, white females, African Americans, and gays and lesbians. Together chapters 6 and 7 build the companion's awareness of the context and social impact on persons' lives and spiritual journeys.

Chapters 8, 9, and 10 focus on particular spiritual dynamics in the life of a Christian. Chapter 8 develops a psychological understanding of guilt and shame as derived from familial, systemic, and social conditioning; discusses the masks people wear to hide shame or guilt; and indicates how spiritual companioning effects healing of unhealthy shame and guilt. Chapter 9 develops a theological and psychological understanding of sin and forgiveness that helps the companion to walk with another through appropriate healing, reconciliation, and inner peace. Chapter 10 highlights the work of grief as an essential spiritual dimension of life. It develops a clear understanding of what grief is and the process of spiritually growing through doing the work of grief. The reflection questions and exercises of these chapters help the companion to tap into personal experiences of shame, guilt, sin, forgiveness, and grief and to grow spiritually in the remembering.

Chapter 11 focuses on companionship with those who have been sexually abused. This chapter gives the contextual framework and the spiritual growth dynamics of survivors of sexual abuse. It delineates the role of the spiritual companion and provides practical suggestions for companioning and for the companion's necessary self-care. This chapter also critiques some harmful theological concepts concerning suffering and offers new theological insights for the companion in the ministry of spiritual care. The exercise at the end of this chapter helps the companion become more aware of one's bodied self as good, created, and loved by God.

Chapter 12 reviews the reasons for and the elements to be initiated in the process of termination of a companion relationship. Effectively ending a companion relationship is as important as an effective beginning, which was discussed in chapter 1.

Appendix A describes the nine different prayer forms that are suggested in exercises or otherwise referenced at the ends of chapters. Appendix B provides a plan for setting up a spiritual companion training program within a community. Appendix C details the practicum component of a training program, and Appendix D details the group supervision component.

Partners in Covenant is an outgrowth of a thirteen-week training program called the Ministry of Christian Listening, which I founded in 1990 and codirected in the diocese of Covington, Kentucky, from 1990 through 1995. I began this program in response to the common hunger for spiritual companionship among people in various life experiences. As a medical center chaplain, clinical pastoral education supervisor, spiritual director, and parishioner, I heard the desire for a relationship through which patients, staff, administrators, students, colleagues, coparishioners, and friends could find spiritual meaning and connection within their day-to-day experiences.

I also heard stories of how other faith-oriented people had been guides and companions in people's lives. Some of these guides and companions shared with me their desire to have their gifts nurtured and recognized within the faith community. I knew that there was an absence of such vocational nurturance and training within church communities. The ministry of spiritual care among the laity needed to be revived and nurtured.

During my six-year involvement in the program, thirty-five men and women were trained as spiritual companions who either expanded their ministry by including elements of spiritual companionship, became more effective as spiritual companions, or made themselves available for peer ministry as a volunteer or paid minister. All were Christian yet not of the same tradition. Participants represented different ethnic groups. Some were employed in church-related roles, some in other helping professions (e.g., physical therapy, sign language, hospital chaplaincy, social work). Some were volunteers or new to accepting their Christian ministry of care.

Spiritual companionship training has been provided recently to members of the Resurrection MCC congregation (Chicago) and to students of the Lutheran School of Theology at Chicago during the 1998–99 academic year. The Resurrection MCC congregation established a peer spiritual ministry. The Lutheran School of Theology program responded to the need for spiritual companionship in both the lay and the ordained ministries of the church for which their students are being prepared. In both programs I used the materials of *Partners in Covenant*.

I wish to acknowledge S. Justina Franxman, David Flynn, and Joan Nordloh in appreciation for their colleagueship and collaboration with me as codirectors. I am grateful to Bishop William Hughes, then bishop of Covington, who supported and encouraged us in offering this program as a vital part of the mission of the church. I am grateful to Elmer Fischesser and the staff of the Jesuit Renewal Center for sharing their experiences as facilitators of a spiritual formation program, and to Julie Murray and companions who continue the Ministry of Christian Listening program in the Greater Cincinnati area.

I am deeply indebted to and thank Ken Overberg, S.J., for his encouragement, untiring, honest consultation, and meticulous review of the materials of this book. I thank Nancy Nolan, S.P., for her feedback and loving patience with me at the computer. I thank Timothy Staveteig, Kelley Baker, and Ed Huddleston of The Pilgrim Press for their assistance and support.

In all and through all I am grateful to God, Faithful Companion.

Part 1: Anchors of Spiritual Companionship

chapter 1

The Art of Covenantal Partnership

Meaninglessness is a major life issue for our culture today. Both privately and publicly people are experiencing a sense of emptiness and meaninglessness. This void and lack of meaning are created by a disconnectedness between what we do and what we say we believe. This separation of doing and believing is frequently due to a lack of reflection and attentiveness to what we say is important. It is, at times, attributed to a lack of clarity in what we do believe and value. It is generated by a life of doing devoid of intentionality.

People are doing more, yet they identify their lives as unfulfilled or incomplete. They describe themselves as lacking a sense of direction or purpose beyond themselves or beyond social pressures. The doing in our society is often guided by the value of how much one produces or how much one has. Personal achievements and corporate success direct our actions from outside forces of systems and structures while depleting us of conscious choices based on our inner beliefs.

Our world, as a result, is a world of relational tensions. Individuals and communities experience tensions between life and death, reconciliation and hostility, community and individualism, global awareness and single-mindedness. These tensions are felt on every level, and people are straining to be in relationships that are consistent with a deeply felt value or truth about their core identity.

People hunger and thirst for a completeness of life. They reach out for more that is beyond the self or the groups to which they belong. There is a conscious search to clarify one's fundamental beliefs and to integrate belief and action, creed and deed. People thirst for meaning and direction in their personal and community lives. They thirst to become aware of and to participate in a fuller life of integration. They hunger for a greater consciousness of their lived spirituality.

Spirituality is what we do because of what we say we believe. What we profess to believe spirituality practices, and what we practice is what we believe. Whether it is stated or unstated, consciously recognized or not, each individual and each group or system of people has a spirituality. Every action—routine or new—is motivated by a belief in human relatedness and worth and is, therefore, an act of spirituality. A key to spirituality is the belief from which action is motivated and done.

Faith-based communities and individuals believe in the Divine. For Christian communities belief in Jesus Christ activates their spirituality. Meaning making for those of faith is enhanced by a greater consciousness of the Divine Presence within and among human life. Direction and guidance toward a fuller individual and community spirituality are sought from the Divine in human experience. Believers seek to grow spiritually by reflecting upon and being attentive to how God might be acting in human history and how their acting is in accordance with their belief in God and in Jesus Christ.

Divine direction comes through human reality. Karl Rahner teaches that God communicates God's self through the event of the human person.[1] To seek divine direction and guidance, therefore, is to do so through reflection upon human experience. The social and communal nature of the human being indicates that this divine direction is sought within human relationships. One does not ordinarily find divine direction by a life of isolation and private interpretation of the meaning of experience. The human person needs companions on the journey of meaning making and connection with the Divine in the integrating of belief and action.

At different times in life individuals are more aware of a lack of integration than at other times. Certain events or life passages have a greater impact on people, creating for them various degrees of disconnectedness and meaninglessness. These events challenge people to explore previously held beliefs and actions. These events are often the springboard from which individuals and communities enter into a new awareness and aspect of their spirituality.

At other moments people experience a flow of life that is rewarding. Amidst this flow they desire to reflect on their reality and to explore the deeper meaning of life in light of their beliefs about the interconnection of their human experience and divine action. These moments of life are often the leaven from which deeper spiritual growth and integration arise.

At times of both challenge and reward, individuals and communities choose to enter into a period of reflection on and exploration of the fuller meaning of life. At these times people seek a greater consciousness of meaning and purpose that will enable them to integrate their life choices and actions. At these times faith-based individuals and communities seek companions on the journey to facilitate the integration of their spirituality. These individuals and communities desire spiritual companions who will walk carefully with them in order to bring to birth the direction of the Divine Presence in their lives.

The spiritual companionship one seeks is a unique encounter of persons built upon a specific covenant between those involved in the relationship. The context of the relationship is the seeker's experience of life. What goes on in the relationship is a reflection of that experience in light of the seeker's needs and spiritual life. The companion serves as a facilitator of grace and is a person gifted, knowledgeable, and called by the community. The foundational gift of the companion is the ability to practice the art of listening in the presence of the person(s) with whom she or he walks.

Spiritual Companionship

Spiritual companionship is an intentional and mutually negotiated relationship between one person (or group)[2] desirous of bringing to consciousness the Spirit operative in his life and another person who serves as companion or partner on the journey. It is a relationship based on faith in the presence of God through which both partners commit to an attentiveness to how the power of the Divine is active and can become more fully available in the private and public lives of the individual. This covenanted partnership of spiritual companionship is for the growth of love with God, with self, and with others. It is for growing in awareness of the influential force of God in human experience and for making real that force in the action of one's life.

Both members of a spiritual companionship may grow in greater holiness through the relationship, yet the focus of the covenant is on the one being companioned. The role of the companion is as facilitator of grace, of the divine self-communication of God's very self to the other. The spiritual seeker assumes the ultimate responsibility for the journey of his life with and in God within the world. Although therapeutic in nature by the ability to release barriers and to open new life-giving vistas, spiritual companionship is not a replacement for therapy nor is it intended to resolve problems. Spiritual companionship is intentional toward the activity of God in another's life while it rests on the mystery of God's action in a person's history. A spiritual companion partnership provides the possibility for new growth and life to be revealed, for growth in the life of grace. Neither partner knows in advance what is to be revealed. Both partners enter surrendering to the divine activity operative through their relationship of attentiveness and commitment to their roles in the process.

The fruits of being attentive to one's life in God through spiritual companioning are the fruits of the Spirit (peace, patience, joy, compassion, justice seeking). Rooted in these gifts, a person can more consistently choose actions that are integrally connected to one's beliefs. The person growing in the integration of the human spirit and the Divine Spirit acts more justly, loves more tenderly, and walks more humbly with God. On this lifetime journey of graceful development, transformation of self and the world is brought about through compassion and justice.

Heinz Kohut in his theoretical construct of self-psychology describes the development of a bipolar self as necessary to healthy human growth.[3] The self matures, says Kohut, through one's intrapsychic experiences of another person (Kohut's concept of "self object"). These intrapsychic experiences provide the grounding upon which interpersonal functions necessary for the growth of a healthy sense of self are developed and maintained. These experiences are the source of one's values, ideals, and life desires. Two intrapsychic experiences of human development are, according to Kohut, that of being admired or affirmed and that of being connected with an idealized image of another. These experiences constitute two poles within the self that serve as the core places out of which one makes decisions, formulates values and beliefs, and performs actions in relation to others. Kohut names them as the pole of healthy grandiosity and the pole of idealization.

In the early stages of life individuals learn through mirroring that they are perfect and affirmed and valued. As the parent delights in the child and receives her with joy and pleasure, the child takes this positive affirmation and mirrors within herself the same delight. The child feels, "I am perfect and you affirm me." The child incorporates a healthy, positive sense of self (healthy grandiosity) that will be her source of desire and goal setting in life.

As the child grows, she becomes aware of the parent, the other. In experiencing the parent's responsiveness and abilities to meet needs and to do things, the child merges with the parent as an ideal. She idealizes the parent as perfect and responds to the parent. She then adds to her self-grandiosity a healthy self-idealization of the other and feels, "You are perfect and I admire you." This bipolar self is the healthy self in loving relationship with the self and with the other. This loving relationship, then, is the encompassing reality from which the child receives ongoing nurturance and guidance for life. Within the context of this loving relationship the child appropriates values, direction, and guidance for her life.

A spiritual companion relationship provides a similar set of dynamics through which a person comes to a greater awareness of "I am lovable and God loves me," and "God is lovable and I love God." The spiritual companion mirrors divine affirmation of the individual and provides a source of divine idealization by her attentiveness and careful listening. It is within this relational milieu that the individual grows and develops on his spiritual journey of being loved by God and in loving God. Based on this love relationship, one is more attentive to receiving and responding to the guidance and direction of the Divine in the experiences of his life. This loving relationship grounds the seeker in reflecting upon and integrating his life of belief and action.

Companion Covenant

The covenant of the companion relationship is between the partners. It is a commitment of faithfulness to the purpose of the relationship and to the role each partner assumes in the relationship. It is a commitment made with an attitude of fidelity and a realism "to the best of my ability." The companion covenants to be an attentive listener and a loving facilitator of the graced life of the other. The seeker commits to be reflective upon his life and to reveal his experiences for mutual reflection and personal spiritual growth. Both partners commit to the life of the Spirit who has covenanted with them and who is ever present.

This covenant of commitment necessarily is embodied in ordinary details. Specific details of the covenant relate to the form and style of the relationship. The spiritual companionship covenant is made for a period of time (initially six months) during which the persons meet regularly (e.g., once a month) and for a specific amount of time (e.g., one hour) in a designated place that provides an atmosphere of confidentiality, warmth, and sacredness. It is usually initiated by the spiritual seeker and responded to by the companion, although if one is in training, she may initiate the covenant with someone who has naturally sought her out for guidance at a particular time.

At the time of initial covenant making the freedom to discontinue the relationship or renegotiate the form and style is verbally stated. Reasons for discontinuing a companion relationship prior to the agreed upon time period vary. The most common reason is that the one being companioned feels his needs are not being met. The other reason is that the companion has encountered an unresolved inner dynamic and she is no longer internally free to be emotionally available to the seeker. Reasons for renegotiating time, place, or style are often based on what works and what does not work in serving the purpose of the relationship. These should not be changed frequently, however, within a six-month period.

Consistency and regularity are important dynamics for a relationship to develop in trust and openness. Too frequent changes in structural elements can delay or permanently interfere with the primary purpose of the companion relationship. If it is appropriate to terminate the relationship prior to the initial time (six months), there should be as much openness as is safe for the individual terminating in sharing the reasons for such termination. If the companion initiates the termination, she should be very clear to the seeker that the termination has nothing to do with him and that it is an issue for the companion. Otherwise, there is the potential of interjecting a false sense of guilt and negative shame upon the seeker. If the one being companioned initiates the termination, all that needs to be revealed is that it does not seem to be working.

More details may be given, yet the companion ought to be cautious in probing too much. While the beginning companion particularly may feel some shame or embarrassment or guilt, it should be understood that these are real feelings that may hold some spiritual invitation, yet not every relationship is meant for everyone at any particular time in life. Being clear at the time of covenant making about the freedom to terminate dissipates any long-term guilt or self-negation of either partner who has been seriously attentive to the specific relationship.

Another aspect of the initial covenant is a mutually agreed upon format for beginning each session. If entering into a spiritual companionship is new for someone, a beginning framework may be unknown, and the companion can offer suggestions to be tried and altered after the format has been experienced. Suggested ways of beginning a session can arise out of the companion's experience of certain styles that were helpful in her time of being companioned.

Some find beginning with a moment of quiet centering followed by a prayer for guidance and attentiveness to the inner goodness of the other a helpful way to begin. This time of centering may also include a request for revelation of divine direction during the session. Others find that one or both partners offering a spontaneous prayer or reading a psalm or other significant prayer is meaningful to set the stage for their time together. No one format is preferable to another.

Concluding a particular session often takes on its own life in the relational process. Frequently, there is a natural ending about five or ten minutes before the specified end time. The fruits of a particular session seem to be obtained, and there is no more to be revealed at this time. The companion does a check-in by asking the other if there is anything else. If there is nothing else, the companion may offer some feedback and reflection on what she heard being revealed and how she perceived God at work in the life of the seeker. The companion then asks if there is anything the seeker feels significant to pay attention to in the coming days. This is not something big and extraordinary to be added onto one's life, but a focus for the person to continue his responsibility of attentiveness in day-to-day life of growing in God.

If an ending does not naturally occur, the companion facilitates ending the session at the designated time. With about five minutes left in the session the companion identifies that there are about five minutes remaining in the time together. She may affirm verbally what has been heard in the last forty-five minutes, for example, an affirmation of the person's very full life and multiple involvements or an affirmation of the person struggling to trust the companion relationship or God. This affirmation is a feedback and a gathering of the person's revelation for both to reflect upon. The companion checks her perceptions with the seeker and asks if there is anything further that needs to be highlighted from the session. A brief clarification of what is significant for further reflection and/or prayer brings this particular companion time to a close.

A factor in the initial covenant is agreement on a review after the initial specified period of time of the relationship (e.g., six months). There is a checking-in about the relationship between those in partnership. Again, this is primarily for the sake of the one being companioned. How is it going? Does anything need to be changed (frequency of meeting, place, hour of day, focus)? Ought the relationship to continue? This checking-in is usually a brief part of one session. If it is determined that the relationship has fulfilled its purpose and should end, it is good practice to set another time to be together with the realization that this is the last formal companion session. An additional meeting allows the best possible termination process to occur in which both partners have the opportunity to express the meaningfulness of the relationship and any regrets, and to offer a blessing or hope for each other.

Companion Context

The context of the spiritual companion relationship is the life of the individual. It is the narrative story of his present life experiences. The story may be a person's experience of himself in relationship with others or with God. The experience someone chooses to reflect upon may be his grief, inner pain in connection with social or religious injustices, gratitude for God's mercy, or awe at creation's beauty. The person and his story as he tells it are important throughout the relationship. How the story is being told, what meaning the storyteller attaches to the story, what images of the self, of others, of the Divine are being expressed, constitute the context of one's life experiences. This unique context is the one in which God is present for him.

All aspects of life are opportunities for spiritual growth; all are initiators of grace. Failures, successes, crises, losses, life transitions, midlife, and aging are all arenas for spiritual awakening and integration. Equally important is the contextual arena from which the individual has developed as an adult. The dynamics within a family, within a society, and within a church form a multiplicity of interconnected dynamics affecting the individual in his present life experiences and desires. The formative images and symbols one has learned from his past and has incorporated in his present experiences enhance or distort the life-giving force of the Spirit.

Psychology and the voices of men and women teach of the different images of the self that each has incorporated into life. Cultural, class, racial, and sexual differences and values add to the uniqueness of the context of each person's history and present experiences. Knowledge of addictions, oppression, abuse, mental illness, and learning disabilities points to the relational issues that affect a person's concept of all other relationships including that with the Divine. Each individual story is the story of a "soul" on a journey embedded in the context of certain realities. Each is the particular and unique context of spirituality being revealed in the here and now of that person's life.

The contextual material as presented may be similar to that presented in a therapeutic counseling session, yet the focus of spiritual companionship is different. A holistic model of counseling contains healing, sustaining, reconciling, and guiding, as does spiritual companionship, yet does not always make explicit the being in God that is specific in the companion relationship.

Pastoral counseling can focus on the counselor as the helper whereas the spiritual companion relationship is recognized as a vehicle of grace in which the movement of God is the primary helper. Therapy assists an individual in becoming a self-differentiated person, in discovering one's uniqueness as an autonomous person. The spiritual companion relationship facilitates the individual in becoming a person in relation with the Divine. Therapy may (and often does) enhance indirectly one's spirituality, but this is not the focus of a counseling relationship. A fundamental trust in a transcendent relationship is implicit in spiritual companioning, and its focus is primarily one's spiritual life. The contextual material of the seeker is viewed in light of divine love and grace.

Resistance to the exploration of divine activity is common, particularly as the companioning relationship is building in trust and safety. This resistance is to be reverenced by gentle acceptance as part of the person's story in the present time. If the resistance persists after several sessions, the companion's naming it for the seeker can be a helpful tool in dealing with his awareness and reason for such resistance to God in his life.

Companionship in prayer life is sometimes the goal of the spiritual seeker. The story of a person's prayer life becomes the beginning context for the relationship. If someone wishes to engage in formal prayer throughout the session, he may be seeking a prayer partner, not a spiritual companion, and the purpose of the relationship must again be clearly defined and agreed upon. One's prayer experiences are important elements that enter a companionship relationship yet serve as the contextual material from which the revelation of God is sought and applied to one's life and action.

Relationship Focus

Throughout the relationship, the companion maintains the environment of a loving relationship that grounds the work of the other during their time together and in between meetings. The undergirding force is the movement of the Spirit in the life experience of the other. The ultimate aim is to assist the integration of one's belief and action, to enhance one's spirituality. There are various avenues in this lifelong journey, and different avenues are taken at different times and moments of the journey. All avenues with an intention toward spiritual wholeness are sacred ground.

People enter a spiritual companion relationship with different needs, at different places on the journey. Some have a specific focus; others come with a more general agenda. Over a period of time new and different needs may emerge as they grow in the spiritual life. Therefore, what goes on within the meeting between an individual and the companion varies in focus and content depending on the individual and his journey. The length of time for a particular focus may be short or long. A companion session may incorporate more than one focus, depending on the readiness of the individual and the connection of one focus with another.

For example, introducing an exploration of one's image of God may be appropriate after several sessions in which there were clarification and affirmation of one's experiences and feelings. Yet introducing one's image of God may be helpful in the same session in which the seeker is hesitant to accept his fear or anger in making a decision. The seeker may image God as not accepting of him as a person who is feeling fear or anger. He may also image God as unavailable to hear his fear or anger.

One event that happens in the relationship is the affirmation and clarification of one's experience. Through feedback and reflective listening, the companion helps the individual to reflect upon and to clarify his experience so that a mutual affirmation of that experience is recognized immediately or over a period of time. For example, the person who may be experiencing multiple stressful events may be initially focused on the causes of the stress rather than on himself as a person who is stressed. How one sees oneself in life's experiences is an important element in choosing how one acts.

Validation of one's experience through affirmation and clarification may shift the focus of the companion relationship to expression of feelings and self/other images. The companion gently invites the individual to express feelings about himself and others associated with that experience. Further exploration happens on the images of oneself and others as expressed in the feelings. For example, the person who is stressed may feel isolated, abandoned, sad, angry, or justified. He may see himself as worthless, powerless, or born to suffer while perceiving the other as better than he is. What one believes about oneself and others is expressed in feelings. What one believes informs how one acts.

What the seeker believes about himself influences his relationship with the Divine and his image of the Divine. Clarification of the individual's present image of God and how that image of God is operative in the individual's life is another focus of the relationship. This image is reflected upon in light of its life-giving force at this time of the person's journey. The companion also invites the individual to explore other images of God that may be operative yet unnamed in one's life. For example, one may have an image of the God of judgment but be unaware of a faithful God who has been with him through difficult situations. The stressed person may also experience the absence of God but be unaware of God's waiting to be called upon for help. The naming of one's image of God brings to consciousness how one experiences the Divine and how that experience impacts his spirituality.

Grounded in love, the spiritual companion relationship can also focus on challenge and confrontation of negative self-images and destructive behavior. The companion who hears a degrading or punishing self-concept from the seeker's story invites him to reflect upon that image in light of God's love and the companion's love and care for him. She may also notice that the seeker acts in ways that are harmful to himself or others. She will confront him on the destructiveness of his behaviors and ask him to reflect with her about these choices.

A person may desire to change his self-concepts and behaviors, yet he may need a healing and loving environment to move beyond them. Others may be unaware of their negativity but welcome such confrontation and challenge if done firmly and lovingly. For example, the stressed person may be aware of doing harm to his body because of never saying no, and he seeks to explore self and God images around this tendency yet is emotionally stuck to do this on his own. Another person may not be aware of this bodily harm and would be receptive to reflecting on this aspect of being stressed when challenged to do so within the loving relationship of being companioned.

Times of darkness—emotionally barren yet fruitful periods of spiritual growth—and the experience of desert enter into the spiritual journey of life. In such circumstances the focus of the relationship is being with the darkness in a way to prevent the natural tendency to escape or run from the desert. The companion receives the story of darkness, affirms it, and assists in the unfolding of the presence of God in the midst of it. This time of desert invites a careful waiting and attentive presence on the part of the companion who models faith in the value of darkness out of which new light and growth are born. In waiting, the companion provides a hope-filled space for the other to live in the darkness, reflect upon it, and grow from it during their time together and in the daily experiences of such emptiness.

The practice of prayer is a basic component of spirituality. People pray in many ways. Cultural differences, socialization, and gender identities lend to the varieties of the expression of prayer. This story of the seeker's prayer experiences is a vital component of the context of one's life. Persons of Asian, African American, and Hispanic cultures have very different prayer forms from those of the European American person. Sensitivity to these differences is imperative in the relationship and should be affirmed and honored as a vital component of human experience. As well, European American men and women often express themselves differently in prayer. These unique avenues of connection with the Divine are to be reverenced and affirmed.

Reflection on one's prayer as an appropriate expression of one's spirituality is, therefore, part of what goes on within the companioning relationship. Other prayer styles are also explored, and the seeker is guided to practice different styles in response to his need. This guidance is particularly helpful when the usual form of prayer of the person is no longer helpful or limits the individual's awareness of the direction of God in his life. For example, the person who is overly stressed may be engaged in the practice of prayer by saying a certain number of prayers each day. This prayer form may add to his stress if it is viewed as a demand from God or is tied up in his self-worth in being able to do something. An alternative prayer practice may be setting aside a time of quiet without doing anything, entering into the presence of the Divine without working at it.

The Spiritual Companion

Historically, the spiritual friend or companion was thought to be embodied solely in clergy, vowed religious, or those with specific long-term training. This is no longer true. In the renewal of the caring ministry of the church, spiritual companioning is acknowledged as a ministry of the community for the community. This function of pastoral care is recognized as a gift of the community. Women and men from diverse backgrounds and a variety of life commitments are being sought out to walk the path of spiritual growth with another. Their personal journeys and experiences in life have paved the way for this ministry.

Persons called to the ministry of spiritual companionship are being asked to be faithful stewards of their gifts. Some want to respond immediately; others are hesitant. Desire to respond immediately can be a self-affirmation of one's gifts and readiness to commit to this ministry. Hesitancy is normal and quite healthy yet ought not completely deter an individual. In either situation faithful commitment as a spiritual companion requires a period of self-exploration and communal discernment.

Discernment is necessary to discover God's invitation and to surrender faithfully to the stewardship of spiritual companionship. Personal and communal reflection is a vital component in this discerning process. Knowing oneself and how one is perceived within the community crystallizes one's call and one's motive for this ministry of care. Moving into the ministry of spiritual companionship out of a motive of wanting to be thought of as wise, holy, or important is harmful to the community. The spiritual companion is fundamentally motivated by a desire to serve and to be a responsible caregiver among the people of God. The spiritual companion is called by the community, is gifted, and is willing to be a steward of these gifts.

An initial sign of the call to be a spiritual companion is that others request a "listening ear" and share easily and readily with an individual. The individual's ability to listen and to be attentive to another is confirmed by the community's response and initiation toward the person. The person has natural empathy and compassion that attract others to her. Others spontaneously seek her out as a companion.

The spiritual companion is, therefore, a trustworthy person who is accepting and compassionate toward others and toward herself. The companion is "someone with whom you feel free to unlock your heart and trust, and who will be able to help you focus . . . on your spiritual journey."[4] The spiritual companion has the ability to provide hospitality, to provide an emotional space for another to feel at home and sufficiently safe to open his life before the companion. She is comfortable with herself, aware of both personal strengths and areas of life that are not quite together and are still in need of conversion.

A person who has an excessive need to be needed or who needs to control the lives of others or to make them different persons is unprepared to begin this ministry. The person who seeks primary satisfaction for needs of belonging and intimacy from the spiritual relationship is called to discern her readiness for entering into this ministry. Needing to be needed and to belong, having desires to control and to be intimate, are all human needs and desires. An excess of these needs and desires or their misplacement within the companion relationship presents an impediment to the spiritual growth of the seeker. The discerning questions for the companion to ask herself are, "In what ways are these needs and desires being appropriately met, and how does the community experience me in interpersonal relationships around these issues?"

The spiritual companion centers her life not only in belief in the Divine but also in faith-oriented action personally and interpersonally. The individual has a willingness and a deep desire to grow spiritually and to walk with others on their journey without a primary need to solve problems or to take responsibility for others. Another quality of the spiritual companion is a sense of humor, an ability to laugh at oneself and allow others to join in, to laugh with another when invited, and to see the incongruities of life. The spiritual companion is capable of tapping in to her emotions, imagination, and thinking. She is able to accept many personalities and to wait patiently for divine direction. The spiritual companion has a demonstrated capacity to maintain commitments to others. She has close friends and is valued as a community member. She is able to be sociable and to establish a close personal relationship with others and to love herself.

The spiritual companion has had some life experience and has been a recipient of spiritual direction, companionship, or friendship. She has been cared for and is able to be both a giver and a receiver. The companion has a holistic view of the human being and is aware of the interconnectedness of all people. She is able to think and act contextually, to perceive the context of one's life inclusive of diverse relational systems and structures. The companion is socially aware (minimally with an openness to expanding this awareness) of cultural diversity, social patterns of injustice, and social patterns of transformation and healing. General patterns of isolation or excessive individualism in a person's life may be indicative of an inability to be attentive to the relational context of the other as well as the dynamics of the companion relationship. To be an effective companion, one must know what it is like to be in communion with others and with the Other.

The spiritual companion is a person of prayer with a reverence for the mystery of God, of the other, and of all of creation. Forgiveness, guilt, sin, pain, joy, grace, and Holy Mystery are part of the companion's life story. She is familiar with various aspects of life and the particularities of the human situation as they affect one's journey with the Divine in feeling loved and in loving. The spiritual companion has a practical knowledge of theology, psychology, and scripture. The spiritual companion is ready and able to learn and to grow through being affected by the life journey of another. She is also willing to be accountable to a consultant, a supervisor, or a spiritual companion.

The spiritual companion covenants to be a partner on the journey directed by the Divine. In responding to the community, the companion commits to being a faithful partner; she does not commit to being perfect. The companion commits to being an attentive and careful listener. Enhancing one's natural abilities as a "listening ear" includes developing skills, incorporating a basic knowledge of psychological and theological concepts, expanding one's awareness of cultural diversity and social situations, and tapping in to a variety of prayer forms. Yet all of the skills, knowledge, practices, and responses cultivated by the companion are beneficial only insofar as they are grounded in the art of listening.

The Art of Listening

Robert Maloney in "Listening as the Foundation for Spirituality" quotes Dietrich Bonhoeffer on the importance of listening. "The first service," says Bonhoeffer, "that one owes to others in the community consists in listening to them. Just as love of God begins by listening to his (God's) Word, so the beginning of love for the brethren (others) is learning to listen to them."[5]

The art of listening is the centerpiece of the companioning relationship. It is the fundamental disposition of the companion and a key component in the ongoing spiritual development of the one being companioned. On the part of the companion, listening is a form of empathy or interpathy (cross-cultural empathy) in which the person enters into the experience of the other. The one being companioned listens to his experiences not only during the companion sessions but throughout daily living to become more and more aware of these experiences and his participation in them. The listening disposition of the companion and the listening of the other center ultimately on hearing who God is and what God is asking of the seeker. "Listening is that attitude of heart whereby that which is deepest and most mysterious in us remains in loving attentiveness to that which is deepest and most mysterious in God."[6]

Practicing the art of listening is hard work. As a form of empathy, listening requires a certain degree of self-emptying, of letting go of personal stories, assumptions, concepts, and preoccupations on the part of the companion. It requires a certain simplicity of shedding one's personal ways of thinking and acting to enter briefly into the ways of another. Listening carefully often brings into question certain assumptions or ways of thinking that the companion holds as vital truth. The companion, then, enters into her own journey (outside the companion relationship) of dying to self in order to enter into another's perspective.

The companion is aware that she brings into the relationship a personal life story that influences her listening with the other. The hard work is not to deny or ignore one's own story. The hard work is to identify and affirm that story and to work at removing the obstacles in listening with a free inner space to hear the Spirit. This work is recognized through the companion relationship yet is not done during the companion session. The latter is for the work of the seeker and not the companion. If the companion introduces her work, this becomes an impediment to the original covenant made for the sake of the seeker. The companion's growth is done in another covenanted relationship in which she is the seeker of growth.

The hard work of listening includes really being present for the other during the companion session at times when one would rather not. This is exacting and demanding. One may become aware of a sense of utter helplessness or may find the person unattractive, dull, or repetitious. The companion may experience the person as manipulative, self-centered, or making mountains out of molehills in a way that irritates her. The hard work of listening demands that the companion focus on the person and let go of her reactions to the person. Again, the companion enters into her own journey and reflection around these experiences outside the session. These are ever new moments of grace for the companion's growth in spirituality. Her attentive listening and response to these moments enhance her spirituality and, consequently, the effectiveness of the companion relationship.

Listening demands more than one's ears. Listening demands one's heart, one's body, one's gut, one's imagination, one's whole personality. To listen carefully in our society of cultural diversity, abuse, and multiple relational styles takes the form of "contextual listening," to enter emotionally and cognitively into the contextual reality of the other. One listens from an awareness of the historical and present context of the other's life. A Caucasian/European American woman in her mid-fifties companioning an African American woman listens out of the African American woman's context of a history of slavery and violence, and a deep sense of family and of God eventually providing freedom. A person listening to a survivor of sexual or emotional abuse listens in the contextual reality of that individual as one victimized by another and dehumanized from believing in his lovableness and redemption.

Contextual listening calls for what Barry and Connolly term a "contemplative attitude." "Relationships develop," they say, "only when the persons involved pay attention to one another. Contemplation in this sense begins when a person stops being preoccupied with his (her) own concerns and lets another person, event or object take the attention."[7] In listening with a contemplative attitude the companion sets the stage for both partners to attend to God as God is present in the seeker's life events and experiences.

To listen carefully is to ask, "What do I hear?" "What do I hear *now,* in *this* event, *within* myself, *within* the community experience, *within* the life of the other?" To listen carefully also means to ask, "Where am I hearing?" "What feelings are emerging?" "What images are present as the story is told?" It is in listening attentively and contextually that the companion hears what is being revealed. From this stance the companion (and the seeker) speaks words that invite the other to greater conscious awareness and integration of his spirituality of creed and deed.

Questions for Reflection

1. What is your understanding of spiritual companionship and how God might be inviting you into this role at this time?

2. What excites you about being a spiritual companion?

3. What signs (personal and from the community) can you name that indicate an affirmation of you in this ministry of care?

4. What fear(s) do you experience at this time of discernment for or enrichment in this ministry?

5. What person(s) do you need to consult about your preparation or continuation of this ministry?

6. Recall a time you felt unconditionally listened to. What do you remember as important to you in the listener's presence and responses? Was there anything particularly helpful or unhelpful?

7. What prayer, scripture passage, or image comes to mind as you ponder this ministry of spiritual companionship for yourself?

You may wish to write your own prayer or an adaptation of one that is your favorite as a daily guide for yourself.

chapter 2

A Theology of Covenantal Partnership

Persons are formed by their mutual relationships with one another. I am who I am because of a relationship to another, a "you." You are who you are because of a relationship to another, an "I." These relationships are by the nature of the human being intentional; that is, I intend to be in relation with you, and you intend to be in relation with me. This intentionality can be self-centered, other-centered, or a balance of self-other interactions.

Jesuit theologian Karl Rahner noted six basic characteristics of being human. The first five characteristics are inherent in human nature and speak to our human-human encounters that define who we are through relationships. These characteristics describe the human as embodied, spiritual, social, unique, and free. As humans, we are bodied persons who are reflective, in relationship with others, individual, and fundamentally free.[1]

The sixth characteristic of being human is the human's capacity for relationship with God. Rahner names this characteristic "supernatural existential," by which he means that the capacity for relationship with God is pure gift; human nature is graced. God is the Other (the "you") desirous of a relationship with each human person and with all of humanity. God initiates the relationship with each person, with each "I." Without this divine primordial desire no person, no "I," could fully exist. Being truly human includes being in relationship with God. Humanity is formed through its relationship with God and becomes fully human in its becoming more and more responsive to God's covenanted relationship with it.

The core of a theology of spiritual companionship through careful listening is the God-human relationship in every lived experience. This relationship is brought to light through reflection on God's dynamic activity revealed through scripture and through reflection on Jesus' personal and intentional fidelity to his graced nature as human.

God's Intentionality

"In the beginning God created." The creation story in its fullness sets the stage for an understanding of God's intentionality in being in relationship with humanity. God hovered over the vast void, breathed God's very life (the "wind from" or "spirit of God"; Gen. 1:2) into it, creating all that is, including humanity made in God's image and likeness. Then God rested. *Menuha* (rested) actually means that God engaged in purposeful contemplation of all that was. God entered into God's creation, observing its meaning and purpose in relation with God's self. God in contemplation became quiet within God's self to see more deeply into created life. God listened on the last day of creation. God was intimately involved in creation through the act of attentive listening.

The biblical story of Adam and Eve depicts humanity's self-realization of belonging spontaneously to the environment with the ability to reflect on its relationship with that environment. This story, similar to other cultural traditions, speaks to the profound tension within human reality to cope with being with the Divine and being separate from the Divine. This tension awakens to consciousness human identity distinct from, yet created in, the image and likeness of God. In being separate humanity strains toward unity with the Divine. The human condition is constantly being pulled toward a relationship with the Creator whom Julian of Norwich conceptualizes as having created all of creation interwoven in the oneness of divine love. The tension of human reality is toward unity with this oneness, to be reconciled in relationship with the Divine.

The Genesis narrative of human creation recounts how "they heard the sound of God walking in the garden . . . and [they] hid themselves from the presence of God among the trees of the garden" (Gen. 3:8). Aware of their separate identity ("because I was naked"), human beings became afraid of relationship with the Divine. God was present with them, yet they strained to deal with their human reality in relationship with the Divine. Human beings struggle in the tension of accepting God's love and presence in the experiences of being human. Where there was oneness, there is now a "you" and an "I." Human beings grow and develop through their relationship with the "you" of God who has created them in love and for love. This God-human relationship is fundamentally grounded in the pure gift of the divine love to which the human person is connected by the nature of his or her creation. From all creation God intends a relationship with humanity.

Contemporary process theology conceptualizes an immanent nature of God through which God continually lures the human person toward God's self within human experience. God is ever drawing the person toward a positive response to God. The more one is free to respond positively to God's invitation through conscious awareness and choice, the greater is one becoming who one ought to be in unity with God. The self becomes more representative of what is of God. God's covenant draws one into relationship with God in becoming more identified with God in human reality.

Hebrew Scriptures

The Hebrew Scriptures are the stories of a people familiar with God's intimate connection within human experience. The stories—of the Flood and Noah who "walked with God" (Gen. 6:9); of the Exodus people who struggled, listened, doubted, and demanded; of Job who cried out resisting his counselors (unwelcomed); of Ruth and Naomi; of the psalmist; of Judith in fierce battles; and of the prophets—are of a people immersed in a belief in God's presence and dynamic activity in nature (the bush), in events, and in people. Time and time again God's covenantal presence is reaffirmed and reexperienced as the people listen and are attentive within their lived reality. The history of the people of God as recorded in the Hebrew Scriptures tells us over and over again of the God-human covenanted relationship.

The scriptural stories of God's people are not about an easy life; the stories are about humanity's active fidelity to the God-human relationship in everyday lived experiences. They are the telling of people coping with their tension of being in human relationships and in relationship with the One in whose image they are created. The stories are about the hard work of listening and attending to God's everlasting covenant and intimate involvement (graced nature) in the everyday encounters of life. The stories are about a people immersed in the belief of God's covenantal love.

In the Scriptures the Hebrew word *shama* and the Greek word *akouo* are routinely used to express the act of listening. The meaning of these words connotes listening to a person, being in interpersonal communion with someone. The meaning goes beyond the hearing (of sound, of words, of music) to the depth of a relationship, to an understanding of one with another. "Both 'shama' and 'akouo,' in their deepest sense, describe a quality that is integral to all loving, interpersonal communion between God and the human person."[2]

In Deuteronomy one experiences God imploring the people to "listen, O Israel" (Deut. 6:4). And in Isaiah, "Listen carefully to me. . . . Listen, so that you may live" (Isa. 55:2–3). Acknowledging his servanthood with God "in the midst of the people whom you have chosen, a great people, so numerous they cannot be numbered or counted," Solomon requested God to "give your servant therefore an understanding mind to govern your people, able to discern between good and evil" (1 Kings 3:8–9). Samuel proclaimed God's covenantal relationship as he cried out, "Speak, for your servant is listening" (1 Sam. 3:10). Judith before her death exalted God as great and glorious, singing,

> *Let all your creatures serve you,*
> *for you spoke, and they were made.*
> *You sent forth your spirit, and it formed them;*
> *there is none that can resist your voice. (Jth. 16:14)*

The Hebrew Scriptures also set before us God's ultimate desire for humanity in its response to God's covenant. In the book of Deuteronomy one reads "of the covenant that God commanded Moses to make with the Israelites in the land of Moab" (Deut. 29:1). After forty years in the wilderness God covenants again with the people to be their God and they God's people. Within this renewal Moses speaks to the people of their part in maintaining the covenanted relationship and the consequences if they go their own way (Deut. 29:19). He also speaks of God's fidelity even in the midst of their unfaithfulness. Then in Deuteronomy 30, we learn what God asks of humanity within the covenantal relationship. It is a command "not too hard for you, nor is it too far away. . . . It is in your mouth and in your heart for you to observe. . . . I have set before you life and death, blessings and curses. Choose life so that you and your descendants may live, loving God, obeying God, and holding fast to God" (Deut. 30:11, 14, 19–20).

The prophet Micah asked, With what shall one go before God? How shall one respond to God? How does one relate to God from whom one is now separate? What does God require in this covenantal relationship? Micah said that God has told us what is good and what is required: "To do justice, and to love kindness, and to walk humbly with your God" (Mic. 6:8). Micah was aware of God's love and fidelity. He also knew that as a human being, he was who he was because of God. The God-human relationship is lived out within human reality in relationship with oneself, with others, and with God. To do justice is to be in right relationship with all human and nonhuman creation. To love kindness is to act in accord with goodness, to choose the good. To walk humbly is to live in the truth and reality of God's real presence and activity in the here and now. To do justice, to love kindness, and to walk humbly with God mean to develop a habit of promotion of all that is of God and a habit of resistance toward all that is not of God.

Lessons from the Hebrew Scriptures

Reflection on the God-human relationship through the Hebrew Scriptures points to several dimensions in a theology of spiritual companionship and careful listening. First, there is the recognition that God is within all experiences through God's act of creation and contemplation and God's ongoing covenantal relationship with human reality.

Second, God wants life for us, not destruction. God does not send tragedy and suffering, yet God works within our human reality (with us) to bring about good in the manner in which we respond to the evils of suffering and tragedy.

God is ever inviting each person and all of humanity to choose what is life-giving (God oriented). Persons are made for love, for relationship of love for others and love for self. God is love, and humanity is made in the image of God.

Third, where there is action in a person's life, God is most present and active. The choices one makes as a result of listening to God through experiences affect who one becomes; the "I" that one becomes in relation to the "you" of God is grounded in one's recognition of the Divine Presence in human experience.

These theological dimensions drawn from the Hebrew Scriptures are instructive in understanding appropriately the desires of God (i.e., the will of God) within the divine-human relational covenant. Through God's intentional covenant, persons are drawn toward the good, toward what is of God. The purpose of all human life is toward divine activity and oneness with the Divine. Persons are made for love. One's deepest self is created by God and is what dwells in God. The separate identity of the human being places one in tension to choose to say yes or no to the divine activity within all that exists. From this fundamental option individuals and communities determine a path of life in word and deed. From this fundamental option individuals discern the will of God by listening to and attending to the Divine in their human reality.

To obey God, to do God's will, is not to figure out what God would do if God were in this situation or that experience. God is already present. To obey[3] God is to listen attentively to oneself and one's community with the ears of a believer in God's covenanted relationship that invites a yes in action and word. To do God's will is to be truly human in relationship with the "you" that is God as best one can discern in human reality. To do God's will is to live in the tension, straining and groaning toward the restoration of the unity of the God-human covenant.

As our ancestors have taught us, obeying God begins by listening with a belief in God's presence and God's intentional everlasting desire for relationship with humanity. Obeying God means saying yes to the voice of God speaking within and through human reality. To do God's will is to listen and to respond faithfully to the presence of God in relationship with humanity in nature, in events, and in all of human reality. "God's will is found in doing what we want at the very best and deepest level of who we understand ourselves to be."[4] "Obey my voice, and I will be your God, and you shall be my people; and walk only in the way that I command you, so that it may be well with you" (Jer. 7:23). "Listen, so that you may live" (Isa. 55:3).

Reflections on Jesus as Human

The theology of incarnation, God's emptying God's self and entering into human life, is substantive for a theology of spiritual companionship within the Christian community. It is within this theology that one explores the truly human Jesus in intentional fidelity to his graced nature. Through the human life pattern of Jesus, one discovers the deepest manifestation of the God-human relationship.

The Word became flesh. God became manifest in and through human life; God speaks in and through the humanity of Jesus. Jesus is God with us in human flesh, bones, emotions, desires. This Jesus invited his first disciples to "come, follow me." Be my companion, walk alongside me, learn from me, is the invitation to discipleship. Who, then, was this Jesus?

Scripture tells us that Jesus,

> *though he was in the form of God,*
> *did not regard equality with God*
> *as something to be exploited,*
> *but emptied himself,*
> *taking the form of a slave,*
> *being born in human likeness.*
> *And being found in human form,*
> *he humbled himself*
> *and became obedient to the point of death—*
> *even death on a cross. (Phil. 2:6–8)*

Jesus was one who "in every respect has been tested as we are, yet without sin" (Heb. 4:15).

Jesus of Nazareth was male. As a human being, Jesus had strengths, weaknesses, gifts, and limitations. He was a certain height, weight, and bodily structure. Jesus was a person with particular personality characteristics, likes, and dislikes. Born into the context and the faith of the Jewish people, Jesus of Nazareth spoke the language of his culture and was steeped in the Hebraic belief in God's everlasting covenant and presence within human life. Contemporary theological understanding of Jesus' self-emptying emphasizes that he did not have a life plan already worked out. "Jesus emptied himself of anything that would have blunted the full experience of being human in the world,"[5] taking the form of one (slave) who is set apart and servant of another. In his humanity, Jesus participated fully in the temptations, in the sufferings, in the searchings, and in the joys of human engagement in life. Jesus of Nazareth accepted himself fully in his humanity, determining his path of life by the choices he made as one with whom God dwells in his human reality.

Led into the wilderness, into that place of desert and bewilderment, Jesus experienced profound temptations of power, wealth, self-preservation, and who knows what else. In the famine and sweat of discernment Jesus resisted the invitation to break with God's covenantal bond with humanity. In his human reality Jesus listened to his experience and to God within that experience. In listening Jesus chose to remain faithful. He began his public life as recorded in the Gospel of Luke by listening to the Word of God (Luke 4). Jesus knew in the depth of his being what his ancestors knew and believed as he proclaimed that "the Spirit of God is upon me, because God has anointed me" (Luke 4:18).

Throughout his human life Jesus experienced struggles, doubts, fears, compassion, and passion. Jesus felt and expressed anger, hunger, sadness, sorrow, disappointment, and the human feelings and desires associated with loving friendships with men and women. Jesus felt a special closeness to Martha and Mary, to Peter, to the apostles and the disciples. Jesus knew the experience of oppression and rejection and all the feelings, thoughts, and desires associated with the society in which he was engaged. Jesus' heart desired to gather together the children of Jerusalem "as a hen gathers her brood under her wings" (Matt. 23:37). Jesus also felt the call to greatness in his own merit: "Many will say to me, 'Lord, Lord, did we not prophesy in your name, and cast out demons in your name, and do many deeds of power in your name?'" (Matt. 7:22). Jesus engaged fully in a life of responsibility through listening to his world, to himself, and to God and acting according to what he believed and heard.

The Christian Scriptures teach us of Jesus as one who listened attentively to the woman caught in adultery, to the Pharisees and lawyers, to the Samaritan woman at the well, to Mary Magdalene, to those seeking healing and the restoration of life. They teach us of Jesus' passionate prayers, listening to and sharing with God his experience of life while seeking direction in being faithful to the covenant.

The Christian Scriptures recount for us Jesus' actions, actions often contrary to those of the society, that came from his listening to human reality and his listening to himself in communion with the Divine. Jesus responded with compassionate love to the woman in adultery, confronted the Pharisees and lawyers, received and offered life to the Samaritan woman, and healed. Jesus not only taught in words to love one's enemies; he also taught by loving his enemies. Jesus looked lovingly on Judas. Jesus' choices carved his life's pattern, a pattern of fidelity to himself as created in covenantal relationship with God in and through his human reality. "Blessed," Jesus reminds his followers, ". . . are those who hear the word of God and obey it" (Luke 11:28). The word of God for Jesus is in and through his lived experiences.

The Christian belief in Jesus without sin does not separate Jesus from human reality. Nor does it make Jesus into someone who in his humanity knew that he was Divine. The revelation of Jesus through scripture as a person without sin is of one who always chose to say yes to God in every circumstance and situation within the context of his time, culture, and lived human existence. Jesus' authenticity was his fidelity to who he ought to be in choosing what he ought to do.

Jesus, for Christians, is the ultimate revelation of the truly human in covenantal relationship with the Divine. The revelation of Jesus is, indeed, the revelation of divinity to humanity, that he is truly God. Jesus is also the revelation of humanity to itself; he is fully human. Jesus' full humanity is the revelation that human sin is embodied in humanity's rejection of the truth of its humanness. Jesus is fully human without sin precisely because he accepted his human condition. Accepting his humanity, Jesus shared in all dimensions of the human condition from birth to death and changed the sinful nature of creatureliness that rejects its own human reality. Jesus' experience was human. Jesus' revelation of the truly human is in the very acceptance of that humanity in its reality.

In the fullness of his humanity Jesus shared himself in relationship with others. Not only did he listen attentively to his experiences and those of others in obedient relationship to the One he called "Abba." Jesus also passed on what he had come to know through his heritage, his personal reflections on the Hebrew Scriptures, his own experiences, and his life of prayer. Jesus' human vulnerability included his sharing with others like himself, those with whom he shared embodiment (flesh). Jesus was not above his co-humans; he was one with them in disclosing what his humanity taught him about himself and about his relationship with the Divine. He said, "I do not call you servants any longer, because the servant does not know what the master is doing; but I have called you friends, because I have made known to you everything that I have heard from my Parent. You did not choose me but I chose you" (John 15:15–16).

Lessons from Jesus

Reflections on Jesus' personal and intentional fidelity to his graced nature as human reiterate those learned from the Hebrew Scriptures, which Jesus incorporated. They also point to and expand several essential elements in a theology of spiritual companionship.

First, and most basic to a theology of spiritual companionship, is the recognition that the Spirit of God guides and is the root of the companionship relationship. The relationship in its intentionality to discover God's activity is grounded in and fostered by a recognition of the work of the Spirit within the relationship itself.

"Where two or three are gathered in my name, I am there among them" (Matt. 18:20). To follow Jesus' path to full humanity is to begin with a profound acknowledgment of one's covenanted relationship with God and giftedness in the living Spirit of God. Spiritual companionship is built upon the desires of both partners (with special emphasis on the part of the one being companioned) to live spiritually within their world through the transforming guidance of the already present Spirit. Listening to the Spirit is essential.

Second, spiritual companionship is a response to follow Jesus, to walk alongside him in his humanity. That is, to be Jesus' companion is to engage responsibly in one's lived experience, to be open to all that is human—emotionally, cognitively, socially, bodily. Feelings, thoughts, social relationships, and bodily experiences can be the word of God that one listens to and attends to within the spiritual companion relationship.

Jesus' weeping over Jerusalem and his desire to gather the people to wholeness in him were born out of deep feelings and a deep knowing of what society ought to be. Jesus' love for Martha and Mary and his grief at the loss of Lazarus motivated his actions to be with them as much as his anger motivated his response to the money changers in the Temple. God speaks as well in dreams (in the day and in the night), in groups, in conflict, in collaboration, in the dynamics of the spiritual companion relationship, in all that is human. As Jesus teaches, one does not ignore or disassociate from but moves through the deepest of pains and sufferings, of unknowing and confusion in listening to and discovering the will of God in life. Jesus' entry into the joys and into the celebrations of people's faith that led to their healing speaks to the discovery of divine activity in times of happiness and peace as well.

Third, reflection on Jesus' humanity points to his self-acceptance in his state of humanness. A gift—and a challenge—of a spiritual companion relationship is the empowerment of one in self-acceptance in and through a personal human history. This self-acceptance is not always easy and includes, at times, a struggle of self-love. A history involving the evils of others in a society of domination, oppression, and abuse makes it difficult to accept human reality. The companion comes to the relationship with a sense of the self as loved and lovable while attentively entering into the context of the self-identity and relationship of the other.

While grounded in the context of the God-human relationship, the spiritual companion relationship evolves within the social and familial history of the life of the other. Jesus, who was grounded in love, called forth persons to love themselves and others. Jesus reversed the societal messages given to those outcast, tormented, and scapegoated by society. Self-acceptance not only enables individuals to be more revealing in the companion relationship. Self-acceptance also allows greater openness ("nakedness"; Gen. 3:11) with God, to let God see them and love them as they are. Jesus' self-acceptance of his humanity as he experienced it in all its vicissitudes opened him to the fullness of that humanity created in and with the Divine.

Fourth is the personal attentiveness to one's inner life outside as well as within the spiritual companion relationship. It is essential that the companion listen in prayer and quiet contemplation to her experiences of the Divine in her life, in the life of the companioned relationship, and in the life of the other. Both partners must engage responsibly in contemplation outside the specified encounters of the relationship. The companion cannot give to others what she does not personally possess.

To be in relationship with one seeking to live more fully in saying yes to life, the companion must be consistently attentive to the divine pull toward goodness and to the personal tension of living human reality. Both partners in the spiritual companion relationship must enhance the ability to reflect upon oneself in relationship to the self, to others, and to God.

Fifth is the sharing of the fruits of one's reflection with others walking the path of human fullness. Self-disclosure of what has been learned in living life is essential for the growth of a life in and with the Transcendent. Self-disclosure within the spiritual companion relationship involves both partners. If one is to discover God's activity (the word of God), personal reflection on one's experience is necessary. Spiritual companionship brings these reflections into a peer relationship within which further reflection and discovery occur. In order for the relationship to develop, the seeker must disclose himself and his experiences; he must be self-revelatory as honestly and forthrightly as one can be.

To grow spiritually through relationship with another, the seeker discloses who he is (in feelings, thoughts, actions) in order to become more of who he is becoming. Equally important is the companion's disclosure as she listens and enters into the relationship. The companion brings the fruits of reflection and prayer on her own life experiences, on scripture, on the human condition, on the lives of others (foremothers and forefathers, others with whom she has companioned). She listens with a discerning ear and discloses what she may be hearing in the seeker's life based on her knowledge, feelings, and instincts to assist the seeker on his journey. The companion, as peer and friend, makes known appropriately what has been made known to her through a life of contemplation.

Following Jesus means taking on a life of fidelity to the God-human relationship in the best way that one can within one's reality. Following Jesus means becoming one with God in all that one does and in who one is becoming. It means fidelity in being in relationship with God. Following Jesus is being truly human.

Psychological Perspective

Spiritual companionship is an encounter of human persons in their maturation and growth toward becoming more fully human in the here and now. The study of human experience demonstrates that there is an inseparable connection between psychological development and spiritual growth. Neither of these approaches does justice to an understanding of human development without the incorporation of the wisdom of the other. Other chapters deal more extensively with some psychological perspectives operative in one's life and in the spiritual companion relationship. For the sake of fairness to the interconnectedness of spiritual and psychological growth it is important to describe briefly one psychological perspective relevant to the theology of spiritual companionship.

Roberto Assagioli in his model of psychosynthesis identifies the central core of the human psyche as the place of love, justice, harmony. The true self, the fully human personality, exemplifies these characteristics. The process of human maturation is, according to this model, the integrating and incorporating into one's conscious personality this true self from which one acts.[6]

Individual self-awareness is a small fraction of who one really is as a human. As experiences are assimilated, there is within the psyche an inner pull toward becoming more of the true self; there is a pull toward the center of harmony and wholeness. With every experience there is a possibility within the human psyche for a more expanded self-awareness that is then reflected in one's personality. Human growth, in the psychosynthesis model, is an openness to this inner dynamic toward the true self of harmony, love, justice. The goal of human psyche development is thus the bringing to fullness the true self as human.

In the theology of spiritual companionship the inner dynamic of the psyche is the divine activity of all persons created in the image of God. It is the human being's inner orientation toward the good maintained by God's intentional covenanted relationship with humanity. The psychological construct of the psyche's pull toward the true self is understood theologically as the lure of God drawing the human person toward God's self, toward unity. The more one becomes who one ought to become as exemplified in Jesus, the more one moves toward harmony, justice, and love, that which is fully human. All of human becoming is toward unity, toward Oneness.

Conclusion

The theology of spiritual companionship is based on relationship. Rooted in God's everlasting covenantal relationship with humanity while reverencing human tension in relationship with the Divine, the spiritual companion relationship is built on the attentive listening to the presence and desires of God in the relational life of the one being companioned. Through careful listening, the companion walks with the other in his growth toward a more fully human life and is, indeed, the embodiment of the loving presence and action of the Divine. The companion relationship is a friendship of people of faith on the human path toward wholeness through which the Spirit of God is at work leading one toward greater fullness as a follower of Jesus.

The spiritual companion relationship grows through the self-acceptance and self-revelation of the other primarily being held in loving attentiveness and acceptance by the companion. It grows through an emptiness of both the companion and the one being companioned as together they listen to the voice of God being revealed in the here and now. The companion brings to the relationship her reflective experiences and knowledge of the God-human relationship, yet lacks knowledge about how God might be active and revelatory in a person's life. Through the relationship of careful listening, the person ascertains the fullness of God in human reality, and the person becomes more fully aware of one's choices in the path of a life lived in obedience to God.

The theology of spiritual companionship sets the relationship in mystery, in the revelation of the Word of God in the fullness of humanity at a particular time of history. Through careful listening and faith-filled attending within a peer relationship to the seeker's human experiences, one becomes more fully human. Through the intentionality of the partners to be in a relationship, to search together for the word of God, and to grow in love as Christ loved, one becomes more of who one ought to be.

Questions for Reflection

1. How has God been active in your life?

2. What is your understanding of the will of God? In what way does the reflection on the will of God presented in this chapter challenge or affirm your understanding and experience?

3. As a spiritual companion, do you experience yourself open to the Spirit of God as guide? Do you perceive any blocks to this openness within your personality or history?

4. Are you a person who endures or embraces pain, suffering, joys, and celebrations? How will your response to life's realities affect your listening attentively and accepting the responses of others?

5. Can you honestly allow God to know you as you are; that is, do you accept yourself in who you have become through your particular journey?

6. What is your practice of contemplation, of reflecting on your reality?

7. What does following Jesus mean to you? Is Jesus human for you?

You may wish to take some time and allow yourself to be quiet before God. In this notice your self-disclosure before God. Are you able to allow God to accept you in the fullness of your humanness? In a notebook or journal that you will dedicate to reflections on your spiritual journey, answer the following questions after your period of quiet:

- What is on your mind and in your heart? Is there a particular word, phrase, or concept that particularly struck you in your quiet time? Is there a certain thought that emerged? Are you peaceful? Sad? Loving? Confused?
- What do these thoughts and feelings say to you?
- How was God with you or absent from you? What image of yourself and God did you have?

Allow yourself to be present to whatever is happening. Is there anything new you had not noticed before? Is there anything affirmed that you had noticed?

At another time period, you may also want to write your theology of spiritual companionship in response to your prayer, your Christian foundations, and the context of this chapter.

chapter 3

Effective Listening to the Companion and God

The fruits of good listening are many. One feels respected, in a place of unconditional acceptance. There is often a felt sense of being brought to a new place of birth within oneself or of being released from internal obstacles because of a safe and receptive environment. Feeling trusted and valued as a person with particular experiences evokes an energy that opens one to meet life's challenges in a free and hopeful way. A bridge is built between one's internal life and external life that enables growth in and through one's experiences. Good listening opens up, whereas the opposite closes or oppresses.

How does one listen within a relationship of spiritual companionship? What does one do, if anything, to assist in interior and exterior transformative growth? What does one listen for that makes the relationship mutually transformative? What is really involved in effective listening as a spiritual companion?

The spiritual companion is primarily an involved active partner whose task is grounded in the way and the what of listening. One is an involved partner by being attentive and actively engaged in the relationship without losing the unique focus of the relationship. The companion is active in being affected within the context of the relationship and acting responsibly in the way one responds within the relationship. Through effective listening, the companion creates a growth atmosphere, an interpersonal climate in which the other becomes progressively freer to assume responsibility and to take greater initiative in one's spiritual life.

The way and the what of listening are incorporated in seven basic elements of effective relational ministry. These elements are presence, reflective listening, empathic responding, understanding, confrontation, use of self, and discernment. The first four are present in every companion encounter; the last three are introduced after mutual trust and basic empathy are established within the relationship. Incorporation of these elements enables the focus of the relationship to be on the inner life of the seeker and his spiritual development.

Presence

Presence is the state of being in which one focuses totally on the here-and-now moment. The companion brings to the relationship an attitude and a sense of being present that provide an atmosphere of emotional safety and hospitality, a place for the other to be as one is. Doing this requires a receptivity of the who, what, and how of the other without placing moral judgment or moral implications ("You did *what?*") on the individual and his behavior; a judgmental attitude is inappropriate. Presence is the "being with" another, an attentiveness to the other in his reality.

Included in being present is the ability to bracket off one's concerns, worries, mental occupations, loves, and self-absorption. Bracketing is a mental setting aside of personal life concerns for the sake of entering into the context and personal life of the other individual. These personal life concerns will be there ready for attention when one is free to deal with oneself; they are not lost.

A companion's presence emerges from both an interior and an exterior silence through which one waits in quiet readiness (as opposed to passivity) to receive the other, verbally and nonverbally. Out of this presence the companion will sense the pace and the timing for entering into the dialogue and for inviting further exploration and growth.

Certain signs for personal reflection are clues that one needs to be more actively present within the relationship. Some of these signs are losing track of what has been said; wandering off mentally; fidgeting; having another conversation in one's head ("How will I respond?"; "If only she were more prepared"; "As soon as this is over I can take a walk"); and experiencing greater than usual energy or lack of energy (if tired beforehand, do something to help one pay attention—drink coffee, ice water, etc.).

The dynamics of transference and countertransference generally occur in any helping relationship and gradually develop over a period of time in a close helper-helpee relationship. They more frequently occur within a psychological relationship in which the counselee grows significantly through focus on the counselor-counselee relationship. They are less frequent in a spiritual companion relationship where attention is given to the human-divine relationship, the companion's attentiveness is relatively transparent, and the sessions are separated by a longer period of time (once a month). The dynamics do occur, however, and the companion's alertness to the clues associated particularly with unhealthy countertransference is important.

Transference is the unconscious transferring of specific feelings onto the companion in whom the seeker has invested certain qualities and attributes pertaining to his parent or other significant person in his childhood. Transference happens in spiritual companioning when the companion is seen as authority (knows truth for the other), is perceived in a parental role, or is set apart as more spiritually advanced by the seeker.

The very nature of the relationship itself sets up transference, which can have a positive or negative effect on the fulfillment of the specific goals of the relationship. Transference is not to be confused with a person's way of relating, which psychology calls "parataxic distortion." This latter happens rather quickly in a relationship and is derived from a specific form of prejudice and stereotyping through which an individual has a predetermined pattern of relating to persons with certain characteristics or external attributes. It is manifested by a reaction to an individual whose actions or appearance is misconstrued; a reaction is distorted in response to the present reality.

For example, a companion's (or a seeker's) mannerism of tapping her fingers while being attentive may unconsciously evoke a hostile reaction from the other; the tapping triggered a response unrelated to the person doing the tapping. Certainly, more profound distortions happen and can be associated with a person's history or trauma. If upon reflection the companion is unable to let go of her prejudice for whatever reason, she needs to terminate the relationship. If the seeker's reaction is distorted and the companion is unable to help him move beyond this reaction to her, the seeker should be encouraged to seek a different relationship. Referral for psychological counseling may be appropriate in these circumstances for either partner or for both, depending on the situation.

Countertransference occurs when the companion relates unconsciously to a seeker as if he were another person; the companion displaces emotions or presumptions onto the seeker that originate in another relationship. Countertransference in spiritual companioning also occurs when the companion's personal needs are interjected into the relationship. A need to care for others, for example, can control one's judgments and ability to listen carefully; the need to care may precipitate a disrespect for the other's growth and lack of conformity to the companion's expectations. Countertransference is often evoked by the transference of the seeker unto the companion. A companion who has a high need to parent others will be very responsive to the seeker's transference of the parental role onto her.

Clues associated with a companion's unhealthy countertransference are as follows: being preoccupied with thoughts of the seeker; fantasizing about one as an intimate friend; creating opportunities to elicit praise or approval; always trying to praise the other; and delving unnecessarily into the other's psychosexual development.

A good method of readying oneself for active presence is taking a few minutes before entering into the spiritual companion relationship in which to quiet oneself, invite God to hold any personal concerns for the hour, and open the self to be receptive and present. This method then requires trusting God's favorable response to the invitation. Through this preparatory method, the companion empties the self of any conscious barriers that could block a free and unconditional acceptance of the other. The companion makes room within oneself to enter into the world of another from which understanding is made possible.

In the beginning of the relationship the companion seeks certain basic information: what the person hopes for; what led the person to seek spiritual companionship at this particular time. Such information can be obtained by asking, "What would you like to share with me as we begin?" or "What would be helpful for me to know about you, about your desires for spiritual companionship?" These questions put a focus and perspective on the relationship from which careful listening and transformative growth in God emerge.

As the relationship moves beyond the initial stages of covenant making and getting acquainted, the companion's quiet presence may provide the space for the other to begin sharing. Depending on style and personality types of the persons in the relationship, one may find that a simple "How might I be with you today?" or "What would you like us to focus on today?" is an appropriate invitation to begin. The companion avoids asking *why* questions ("Why have you come today?") because the nature of such questions evokes a degree of guilt and judgment in the one being asked. The skill of a spiritual companion is in the ability to create and maintain a free and safe space for the other to discover and follow one's personal path to full humanity. This skill begins with a clear sense of presence and openness to the other.

Reflective Listening

Reflective listening is the activity of letting the other know that he or she has been heard, verbally and nonverbally, through words, expressed feelings, and/or body language. Reflective listening brings the thoughts, feelings, and desires of the private world of the individual into the conversation of the companion relationship wherein God's movement can be discerned. Reflective listening confirms that the companion has heard clearly what was said, affirms the seeker, and establishes a trustful confidence in the relationship as a vehicle for personal growth. Reflective listening is a hermeneutical task that leads to the discovery of more and more of the God-human story within a person's life and within the life of the society.

Reflecting what one has heard can be done by paraphrasing; by synthesizing ("You have had many losses lately"); by repeating, slowly and thoughtfully, a descriptive word, phrase, or dominant feeling expressed ("happy"; "life is confusing"; "sad and happy"); and/or by giving a name to an unnamed feeling being expressed (noticing slumped shoulders or clenched fists of the person, "This week's events seem to be weighing you down," or "You seem to have to hold on tightly this week").

Using any of the skills of reflecting is like holding a mirror for the person to look into. Healthy use of the skills avoids a declarative or definitive tone of voice; the other is the only one who can verify what is reflected. Reflection is brief and is inserted periodically in the relationship. Pausing after the reflective feedback offers the individual time and space to "see" more clearly and to test whether or not this is the truth at this time. Pausing also makes space in the relational dialogue for feedback to the companion. Such feedback from the person comes in expressed emotions (person laughs, cries), in verbal affirmation, in further self-revelation, or in a visible change of body language. In the latter case, the companion can seek further verbal feedback by asking, "Have I heard you accurately?" or "Did I miss what you were telling me?" or "Can you tell me if I am hearing you correctly or not?"

The feedback is received and further reflecting continues. Argumentation on the part of the companion (after the feedback, "No, life isn't confusing," one says, "But you just said that") introduces a big stumbling block; reception is the initial key (e.g., "Oh, I am sorry; how would you describe life for you right now?") to empowerment and self-acceptance within the relationship.

Other clues for needed growth in the art and skills of reflective listening are as follows: being unable to let go of a personal agenda in preference to the other's agenda; choosing only certain feelings to reflect (every time anger is used or expressed, the companion ignores it); experiencing inner agitation at the slowness of the other to "get to the point"; making declarative statements; and colluding with the person by focusing on a topic of shared interest (relationship becomes one of two "buddies" in which the companion gets an audience for what she feels strongly about).

Often in the spiritual companion relationship the use of reflective feedback alone is not sufficient. When deep feelings of fear, anger, guilt, love, passion, or sadness, for example, are expressed, these feelings need to be further discussed and their meaning explored for the one being companioned.

Empathic Responding

Empathic responding flows from an attentive presence and is integrated within the skills of active reflective listening. Empathic responding is a caring response to *the person* who is feeling a certain way, to the person who is acting or has acted a particular way. It maintains the focus on the person and avoids responding solely to the feelings, thoughts, behaviors, and attitudes of the other. Such responding grows out of the companion's felt identity with the person as he has been self-revelatory within the relationship. Empathic responding activates the process of growth for which presence and reflective feedback have prepared the way.

> Empathy is sharing another's feelings, not through projection but through compassionate active imagination. Empathy is an intentional affective response . . . the choice to transpose oneself into another's experience in self-conscious awareness of the other's consciousness . . .

enriched between the observer and the observed, but it is based on differences . . . respects the distinctness of self and other and seeks to
enhance rather than diminish these boundaries.[1]

A predisposition of the companion is one of chosen vulnerability, a willingness to be affected (touched, moved, changed, stirred) by the person and
life of the one being companioned. In this vulnerability, the companion
enters the reality of the other person through the imagination (*everyone* has
one, but most need to activate it!). The companion images the personal story
that is being revealed and vicariously experiences (is "being with") the feelings, attitudes, and thoughts of the other person. The story that one is telling
may be from a culture similar to that of the companion or from a cultural
context and worldview very different from one's own. Feeling with and
thinking with the other may require entrance temporarily into a world of
assumptions, beliefs, and values radically different from one's perceptions
and reality. The imagination is the entrance into the life of the other as that
person experiences it; the imagination is the doorway to a felt identity with
another. This is the incarnational reality of companioning, the entering into
the experience of the other for the sake of the other.

Invoking the imagination raises certain feelings of the companion in con-
ceptualizing the here-and-now story of the other. To respond solely out of
these feelings limits a truly empathic response; empathic response includes
personal feelings yet extends to the other's feeling experience. It is important
to listen for and to invite a revelation of feelings by the other. Given a
propensity to reveal thoughts only, the companion may need to assist the
individual in naming and claiming feelings (what Ignatius of Loyola identified as God's vehicle for speaking; what psychologists identify as the place
from which action and change come). The companion must consistently
maintain respect for cultural variations in sharing and expressing feelings.

Feelings are often not named (or claimed) even though the word "feel" is
used. "I feel strongly about equality for homosexuals" (a thought), "I feel
better" (a state of being), and "I feel the system is not for me" (an attitude)
are examples of such word usage. To assist a movement to the feeling(s) that
supports the thoughts, states of being, and attitudes, the companion can
name for the other the four major categories of all feelings: mad, sad, glad,
and scared.

For example, "When you feel strongly about equality for homosexuals
[repeating], do you feel mad, sad, glad, scared?" "When you think about the
system not being for you [paraphrasing], are you aware of how you feel?"
Response: "Mixed." Companion: "Mixed. [pause] Would you say that mixed
is mad . . . ?" Certain stated feelings may mask the real underlying feeling
that one needs to hide. Feelings of sadness, fear, and anger can be masks for
one another; feeling sad may be more "acceptable" than feeling scared or

angry and vice versa. Whatever the reality, the companion receives the person as he presents himself.

The companion, in imaging the here and now of the other, empathically responds out of a threefold dynamic: "my" feelings as I imagine this reality; "your" feelings as you are in the reality and I image that as you have revealed it; "our" feelings that are shared at this moment as a result of your story.

One pitfall in empathic responding is that of confusing or crossing over boundaries. Taking on another's feelings and making them one's own diffuse what is "mine" and what is "yours." The relationship becomes a caretaking one rather than a caregiving one, and identification of the one being served is blurred. On the other hand, fixed boundaries have rigid parameters. The companion is not vulnerable to the person and is untouchable emotionally. There is a lack of connection necessary for growth; there are often issues of power and misuse of authority in these circumstances.

Having permeable boundaries in which both parties maintain their identity, emotionality, and self while being affected and changed (by choice) by the other is the ideal to be sought. Within permeable boundaries there are a fluidity of vulnerability and, at the same time, a personal freedom of choice. Physical and sexual boundaries are also to be considered in light of reverence, respect, and appropriateness. A rule of thumb is this: no one has a right to touch another person or to be close physically to him or her without permission. Presuming and holding someone's hand may (or may not) be intrusive to that person. The questions for the companion are: Whose need is it? Has my behavior (words, actions) demonstrated a furtherance of this person's freedom and growth? Did I respond out of a felt identity with him as separate from me? Do I truly care for that person as a person created by God, good and lovable?

Understanding

Understanding is the coming to know how the other perceives reality based on his own frame of reference and not on the companion's frame of reference. Understanding involves coming to know what something is like *for the other.*

Understanding involves letting go of certain ideas and concepts about other persons because of class, gender, culture, sexual orientation, race, or prayer styles. Understanding sees the other as a person rather than "another man," "a feminist," "a homosexual," "a typical African American," "a conservative," "an emotional Hispanic," or "an old-time Catholic." Labeling in this manner is often a sign of prejudice in which the companion has an uninformed attitude or feeling; the companion has already judged and formed an opinion about the other prior to coming to know that person for who he is and has become. The companion's projection inhibits understanding of the other as a unique person.

To understand the seeker, the companion endeavors to become aware of her own prejudices and to work at letting go of them in order to hear and receive the other in truth. This letting go involves a certain interior emptying of the self for the true identity of the other to be received. The process of letting go happens both during a spiritual relationship session and in between as the companion becomes aware of her projections and chooses to let go of them.

Labeling (and subsequent projections) may also be indicative of the companion's lack of awareness of the larger systemic issues associated with her position and those of the seeker in society, whether of class, culture, gender, race, sexual orientation, or religious affiliation. Understanding involves an awareness of the social systems and structures in which the spiritual partners participate and how these have affected each one regardless of the differences or similarities of their lives. Examples include one's being aware of the domination and misuse of power of white North America, of economic advantage, of church structures, and of cultural norms that have oppressed and excluded others in thought and action. Other examples include systems and structures of the less dominant and powerful, Hispanics, African Americans, open-door congregations, gay and lesbian groups, feminist, and womanist. This wider systemic awareness of herself, and the other, enables the companion to develop a more effective relational space for the seeker to grow spiritually on his own path.

A companion participating in the more dominant systemic structure (e.g., European American, hierarchical church position, white male) listening with someone of less dominant systems (gay, laity, female) brings to the relationship a historical inequality of power between the companion and the seeker regardless of individual encounters between them. This systemic relational dynamic is operative yet often unspoken insofar as the seeker and the companion have entered openly and sincerely into relationship. It is present because of the very nature of systemic issues of which we are all a part. A companion who has not reflected on these "built in" dynamics (albeit unconsciously) is unaware of the impact of her responses and presence on the other by the nature of who she represents systemically. She will also be unaware of her behavior that may reinforce the domination and power of one over another.

Equally significant is the listening for understanding of one who has been the recipient of societal oppression and/or dominant power, especially when the seeker is from a dominant system and social structure. A companion engaged in such a relationship who has not reflected intentionally and systemically overlooks the importance of the unconscious dynamics affecting the relationship and growth of the other. She will also be unaware of any inferior attitude that prompts her behavioral responses.

Being aware of the systemic issues allows the companion to understand through unbiased listening not only the fuller context of the individual, but also the unspoken dynamics that enter the peer relationship through the projection of biases and prejudices. Awareness brings an understanding insight into one's behavior as it may be perceived by the other as well as a broader and more inclusive frame of reference from which to come to know the one being companioned. However, this awareness does not presuppose that the companion now knows the other because of her intellectual study of social systems. The companion brings this awareness to the relationship as a resource from which to listen attentively to how the seeker understands himself personally and socially. The companion utilizes this awareness as she reflects on her functioning and on the dynamics occurring within the relationship.

Another stumbling block to true understanding is that of collusion. Here the companion is of the same frame of mind (and emotion) relative to a particular topic or response/reaction as the one being companioned. Collusion occurs most frequently when the seeker brings up a topic or issue that is unresolved in the life of the companion.

For example, the seeker describes a recent corporate board meeting that "went nowhere." He also expresses his deep frustration with the ultraconservative chair of the board. The companion is exasperated by committees and groups that "go nowhere" and with leaders who have no creativity toward change. She gets caught up in the topic of conservative no-progress groups and responds, "Groups like that drive me crazy. Aren't they awful?" And the conversation proceeds on this topic and away from the seeker, whose feelings and responses were significant to his experience. Instead of responding empathically ("You must find it difficult to stay in the room") or exploring the meaning for him more fully ("Would you like to explore your frustration?") for understanding, the companion colludes with him about conservative people and meetings. Collusion occurs around systemic similarities as well (e.g., a female companion may collude with another woman who is experiencing some form of exclusion in her pastoral position).

Recognizing and naming prejudices, projections, systemic issues, and collusion enable the companion to claim them and then to act accordingly to change for the sake of the companioning relationship. This process of naming, claiming, and acting is a responsibility in all dimensions of the companion's self-growth as an effective minister of care. True understanding of the other is possible only insofar as the companion understands herself and what she brings consciously and unconsciously to the relationship.

As Thomas Moore in *Care of the Soul* has reminded us, it is getting underneath the masks that is the place of care of the soul, the place of spiritual life and transformation.[2] These masks can be the prejudice or projection of the companion as well as those of the care receiver. Lifting the masks of labeling and other masks of invulnerability, power, or prejudice is part of the covenant to which the companion has committed in entering the ministry of careful listening. Imperative in fulfilling this commitment are ongoing personal reflection, consultation or supervision, and spiritual companionship.

Confrontation

Confrontation is the naming of inconsistencies. Confrontation is truth telling grounded in loving respect of one person for and with another person. To confront is to hold up before someone a truth that another has perceived. Confrontation has often been misrepresented as telling someone what is wrong with him, attacking another, having angry outbursts, and the like. True confrontation requires care, love, freedom, and trust of oneself and the relationship. Without these "ingredients" the feedback is potentially domination of one over the other, a win-lose, a my-way or your-way situation. Confrontation is clear and assertive: "Earlier I thought I heard you saying that everything was okay. Now I am hearing you say you are confused. I don't think of okay and confused as going together. Could you help me see how they go together for you?" Another example could be, "You said that God was probably angry with you. I am aware that you are smiling when you tell me. When you think God is angry, do you feel happy?"

Confrontation gives the other person feedback on how the companion is hearing him, yet it is done in a way that offers a freedom of response. He may answer, "Yes, when God is angry, I am happy." This is the truth as the person is aware of it and chooses to respond. Further invitation may ensue to help the companion and the other become clearer about what is happening. "Do you care to say more about how God's anger makes you happy?" Confrontation gently frees the person to come to greater truth about himself. It is an art and a skill pushing the seeker beyond his present point of growth.

Confrontation at the early stages of a companion relationship is used to clarify and to mirror to the other what has been heard. In this early stage confrontation is more closely associated with the skill of reflective listening. For example, a person's stated reason for entering into a companion relationship is to grow more loving toward God, whom he identifies as judgmental. Aware of the contradictory nature of this stated desire, the companion would use this confrontation: "You want to love God who judges you." As trust and empathy have been solidly established within the relationship, the skill of confrontation is applied more directly in holding up for the other his distorted (or at best incomplete) concept of the God-human encounter built on a judgment-love relational dynamic.

Confrontation also invites the person to move from indirect revelation to direct revelation often associated with one's fear (manifested as resistance or defensiveness) of being accepted by the companion or by God. The individual may be jumping verbally from one topic to the other without acknowledging the companion's empathic response to any one topic. In the earlier period of the relationship the companion may inquire if he wishes to explore one of the topics more fully. In the later stages of the relationship after trust has been established, confrontation is more direct in holding before the seeker the underlying messages of his behavior. Confrontation states the pattern of the seeker's behavior with an invitation to discover what lies beneath the surface behavior. For example, the companion states, "I am aware that you are jumping from topic to topic," and then asks, "Is there something you are avoiding today?" or "What does this mean for you?"

Some signs to note in the practice of confrontation are as follows: response of the one being companioned; multiple uses of confrontation in one session; and personal (the companion's) openness to confrontation. If the response is atypical (for that person)—aggressive, angry, shame-based, quiet—the companion's self-reflection ought to be centered on her own manner, tone of voice, word usage, loving care, and trust. If the companion often uses confrontation, perhaps she is off on a personal agenda or is projecting personal desires, confusion, or anger. One's personal openness to confrontation within a caring relationship (or noncaring relationship for that matter) is instructive about how one might use confrontation as a care provider.

The principle of parallel process is to be considered in a caring relationship. How the companion tends to relate when receiving care from another (open, hidden, free, manipulative) transfers into the dynamics in the companion relationship. The companion unreflectively introduces into the relationship an expectation that the receiver respond in either a similar or a completely opposite manner to her as the caregiver. If the companion is more hidden in receiving care, then she may set up barriers for the other to be hidden, or she may "push" the other to be an open book in all circumstances. If the companion enters a caring relationship expecting to be "taken care of," she may approach the companion relationship in a way that fosters caretaking, or she may strongly resist overtures by the other to be taken care of.

Parallel process is a normal reality in any caring relationship. The goal of the effective companion is to become aware of these dynamics and to continue to grow in freedom, presence, and empathic responding in relation to the one being companioned.

Use of Self

Use of self is using one's feelings, thoughts, and history to inform empathic responding within the relationship. This skill arises out of growth in empathy, self-awareness, and personal integration. As the companion images what it might be like for the other, she gets in touch with how it might be for herself in a particular situation. Out of this felt sense of the self, the companion offers a reflection.

As the companion listens, she feels a personal sense of being sad if in the similar situation and responds, "That must be quite sad for you." The companion, feeling sad in entering into the other's story, uses the self to "check out" if that is the emotional response of the other. The companion's feeling response may or may not be that of the other. If it is similar, the companion invites further exploration; if it is dissimilar, the companion must let go and invite the other to share what it is like for him.

A pitfall in using oneself is beginning to talk about oneself. There is a place for self-revelation on the part of the companion ("I remember once being in a similar situation and I recall feeling quite sad; is that how you are feeling?"), yet the context of the caring relationship is not the place for focus on the companion's storytelling or sharing. Appropriate self-disclosure is not talking about oneself; it is sharing what has been learned from one's experience.

Discernment

Discernment is the art and skill of helping the other to separate priorities and to make choices for the future based on resources, past experience, and personal concepts of God, self, and other. In a companion relationship this is often not a major life decision, although it could be. It is more likely to be used at a time when multiple events or feelings are flooding the life of the other.

The companion hears a list of feelings or circumstances impacting the life of the person. After careful and reflective listening through which the person names all that is converging on his life, the companion asks, "Of all these [restating the feelings, events], which one or two seem to be the most important or the most disturbing for you right now?" By this process, one companions the other to clarify his focus and his sense of importance. An individual does not always know which one or two are important; all seem of equal impact. The companion then stays with the person who is experiencing multiple "forces." After some time (many sessions perhaps) the person, in his own readiness, will be able to narrow the focus.

Conclusion

Each of the elements—presence, reflective listening, empathic responding, understanding, confrontation, use of self, and discernment—is unique yet interconnected. The first four are particularly intertwined within each companionship encounter. There is within the relationship a sort of dance or tension of intimacy and distance, of connecting and disconnecting. This same dance happens in humanity's desire to be in relationship with God. We want to be more intimate with God, yet we often fear that intimacy. As life affects human beings, God affects them, and as persons react to life, so they react to God.

The task of effective listening within a spiritual companion relationship is to help the seeker attend to his interior happenings when in the presence of other persons and in the presence of the Divine. Practicing the elements of effective listening turns the companion's attention away from the objects of the other's hopes, frustrations, worries, and cares to the inner events of the seeker's hopes, frustrations, worries, and cares.

Effective listening enables a movement from a surface description of one's experience to the underlying core of life for him. Effective listening enables the partners to grow beyond "just two people talking" to a mutual companionship of two people attending to the voice of God in the life of the seeker. The companion's faithfulness to the art and skills of effective listening allows room for God to be revealed in the life of the other. God invites, challenges, consoles, reveals, and urges reaction and response through the companion relationship.

Questions for Reflection

1. Think of the last two times you were a listener with someone. Using the elements presented in this chapter as a guide, which ones did you use, and which ones might you have used?

2. What element (elements) will you practice particularly this week? When will you practice? (Saying "all the time" may lead to lack of success.)

3. When you listen to yourself, what do you usually hear? Is it hard or easy to listen to yourself? Is there something you would rather not hear? Can you tell God about it?

4. What are you becoming aware of about yourself in the ministry as spiritual companion? Any prejudices, biases, likes, dislikes? Any awareness of your culture and the systems affecting your life?

5. Draw a large square. On the inside write the types of people you let into your life. On the outside write the types of people you generally keep out. What would you need to do to create space for the outsiders?

6. Just *be*. Pay attention to "be still and know that I am with you." Pay attention to your inhaling and exhaling. No judgments. Just attention. When you sense an emptiness, repeat slowly and rhythmically, "Come, Holy One, come," several times. At the conclusion, write down your experiences.

7. What connection is there for you between the theology of spiritual companionship and the art of effective listening?

Record in your spiritual journal your feelings, thoughts, insights, responses, or reactions as you continue in your reading and in being a spiritual companion. Choose a feeling, thought, insight, or response, and enter into a written dialogue with Jesus, God, the author, or someone else. This dialogue is a spontaneous conversation between you and the other. Do not think about what the other ought to say. Allow your inner self to hear the voice of the other. Here is how to do the journal dialogue:

- Write your opening statement as M-1.
- Write Jesus' response as J-1.
- Then, your response is M-2.
- Then, Jesus' response is J-2.
- Continue in dialogue until there is a natural ending, or if you feel you cannot continue, be sure to let your dialogue partner (Jesus, God, author, another) know that you need to stop. Be sure to pay attention to the response given. Write it down.
- Close by praying your prayer of guidance or by any other prayer or quiet being that seems appropriate for your needs.

Be aware if there is anything you need to come back to in your next period of prayer. Do you need more dialogue? Do you need to journal feelings? To what are you being invited?

Part 2: Dynamics of Spiritual Development

chapter 4

Prayer

P
rayer is a fundamental activity in the life of a Christian. "Pray always" (Luke 18:1) is the instruction Jesus gives to his followers. Living in the tension of being one with God and being separate from God, humanity enters into prayer to connect its spirit to the Spirit of God. A life of prayer is the very connection of the ordinary self to the power of God within and in the midst of human experience. To "pray always" is to kindle attentively the flame of the Divine in all of one's human reality.

The Act of Prayer

St. Teresa of Avila described prayer as situated in different layers, castles, or mansions. Ignatius of Loyola spoke of contemplation and three other methods of prayer. Hildegard of Bingen represented prayer in mandala forms and caricatures. John of the Cross identified prayer as a three-tier mountain of purgation, illumination, and union with God. There is kataphatic prayer that focuses on images, thoughts, sensations, and emotions. There is apophatic prayer that is imageless. But what is the act of prayer?

Prayer is a matter of the interior life of a person, a journey within. Initiated by God through God's indwelling presence, prayer is the human encounter with God. When an individual (or community) turns to prayer, one joins with God who is already praying within that person (or community). God is already in relationship with the person (or community) who in turning to prayer enters into relationship with God.

Prayer, then, is a paradox; it is both a gift and something one learns how to do. God who first loved humanity is the Spirit of Love who draws a person to prayer and from whom one learns how to pray, to meet, and with whom to grow in love. The reception of God and growth in love with God require human responsiveness, a being-in-relation with God. As in any relationship that grows beyond the mere existence of two people, growth in the God-human relationship matures through the engagement of both God and the human person. God is ever engaged in human reality. The person engages God through prayer in which one comes to know God, reveals one-self to God, and grows intimate with God. Prayer presupposes that one believes in the presence of God in human reality and is desirous of being in loving encounter with the Divine.

The core of prayer is the act of being still. "Be still, and know that I am God" (Ps. 46:10). Yet prayer is not a private act. In coming to know God in prayer, a person comes to know oneself within the encounter with God, and is transformed by the relationship toward a more fully human life. Prayer transforms the interior life of the individual to live externally in say-ing yes to what is of God. Prayer nurtures the growth of the individual sown with the seeds of divine love from which a hundredfold of loving activity is produced in one's life (Luke 8:8). In its fullness, prayer engages one in an act of co-creation, in the participation of bringing into reality creation in relation to God. Prayer liberates the interior life and the outer world of evil forces, of the powers of humanity that disavow, block, resist, and negate God's loving presence.

The act of being still is not to be equated with a kind of solitude that is the going to a place alone, a retreat center, a hermitage, a place in the woods, a favorite room in one's home. Solitude is necessary periodically in one's life, just as Jesus went away at different times from the crowds. Solitude helps one's constant life of prayer, and in solitude powerful prayer experiences often emerge. The stillness of solitude requires a place set apart. The stillness of prayer requires a journey inward while living a life in relation to the world of people and events. Some are called to a lifetime of solitude, yet most have a life of activity. The stillness of prayer is a quietness of the heart, an interior freedom from the clutter of preoccupations and of the busyness about many things. It is a freedom from the illusions that one is the sole actor in the drama of human existence.

To still the heart is to make space for an encounter with God, to clear one's inner life of all that blocks a connection with the indwelling Presence of Love. Stilling the heart decreases the fires of self-centered living in order to increase the flames of God-centered living. The act of being still demands a letting go, an emptying, of self-centered power and an openness to the influ-ential power of the Divine in human reality. In inner emptiness one meets the loving presence of God.

To be still and know God is not an easy task for anyone. It takes effort. It requires a belief in God's everlasting presence, a desire to know God more fully and to be known by God. It requires the risk of faith that trusts in the power of God's love to maintain the relationship, that God cares enough to remain with one no matter what. The more one knows God, the more one is aware of the self as separate from God yet one with God. The more one knows God, the more one loves oneself as loved by God and in love with God. To know God is to know oneself as truly human.

Moving inward in meeting God, one is drawn by the Spirit to enter more fully into the divine relationship. The prayer of encounter may be one of awe, praise, or thanksgiving as one recognizes the otherness of God. The continuing prayer of coming to know God is one of engaging the Other, of entering into a personal relationship with the Other. Growth in relationships requires mutual self-revelation and response. God is known through the interactive encounter of the self with the Other.

The coming to know God includes the individual's letting oneself be known by God. Prayer involves a person telling God about the self and listening for God's revelatory response. This self-revelation requires an openness and an acceptance of oneself, the presentation of all of oneself—body, feeling, imagination, intellect, desires, culture, environment—to the Other. The stilling of heart in prayer is the very emptying of self in sharing with God all that is the self. Opening oneself in the presence of the Divine, as in any relationship, may be through verbalization or through an interior attitude of total presence of all that one is in the presence of the Other. Attending to God's response within as one presents the self to God enables one to come to know God and to choose to be more fully connected with God.

Pathways to Prayer

The pathways to prayer are as different as the people who pray. Some paths are helpful at one period of life's journey; others are more fruitful at another time. The holistic nature of spirituality and the integration of personality of any one individual warrant a movement from one prayer pathway to another at different psychological stages and at various junctures of spiritual growth.

One pathway is the prayers of others that are often prayers of praise, recognition, or request. They include Jesus' prayer to God, Abba, the prayers of the Psalms, the prayers of Hildegard and of Thomas Merton, Mary's greeting to Elizabeth (the Magnificat), and the prayers of the eucharistic liturgy. Through these prayers, a person who desires to be in the presence of God enters into the words, making them one's own. Utilizing the prayers of others provides the temptation to recite words and not to enter into prayer. In the absence of an awareness of the Other to whom one is praying, the individual is not able to connect with the Divine in one's own way. Requests (including those of intercessory or petitionary prayer) become mere activism when the one "praying" lacks the inner consciousness of a relational dynamic between oneself and God. However, because of the Spirit's praying already, the practice of recitation of prayers can awaken one to the presence of God.

A second pathway is the use of scripture, icons, or nature. This way of praying involves the active use of the imagination. One imagines being present in the scene of the scripture while attending to one's feelings and thoughts, letting the scripture speak personally to him. One focuses on an icon image or on a scene of nature, allowing it to enter into one's being, to speak its message of God's activity. Combined with this pathway of prayer is the incorporation of a mantra. Use of a mantra, the rhythmical repetition of a short phrase, enhances one's ability to be still and allow these images to speak to one personally. A simple mantra is "Come, come" or "Yes, yes." Using a phrase from a psalm or other scriptural passage as a mantra opens one to a deeper awareness of the meaning of the Word of God for him. For example, a mantra of "Hallowed be your name, hallowed be your name" effects the hallowing of God's name in the inner life of the person.

A third pathway is the use of one's bodied self in dancing, in listening to music, in painting, in singing, in forming clay, in moving spontaneously (even walking). This is a powerful pathway often not chosen in a society that values reserve and propriety. This path to prayer activates a person's creative center. Praying through one's physicality, the individual expresses externally what is deepest within him, what is beyond words or concrete structural form. Praying through one's creative expression releases positive as well as negative inner energy. It is an aid for some individuals to become more aware of feelings and thoughts that they are unable to name or are aware of only through physical manifestation (knot in the stomach, stiff shoulders, headache, weak knees).

A fourth pathway to prayer is through talking with God directly. Some people find this prayer form the most helpful. In this prayer the individual, aware of God, enters into a dialogue with God by talking about his day, about himself in the day, about his joys, concerns, worries, about a passage of scripture. One may talk to God, telling God of how hard it is to listen or to reveal oneself to God. "Was I ever caught in a bind today. I didn't have a clue what to do when . . ."; "You know, God, I really want to listen to you. Well, sort of. You see, I am afraid of what you might say"; "Okay, God, it is celebration time. I really love Harriet"; "You say that one must become like a child. What did you mean, God?"

Having thus begun the dialogue, the person continues the prayer by listening as God receives and responds to what has been revealed. One's listening evokes further response that ends the conversation ("Thanks, God, for listening to me") or continues the prayer ("Are you there, God?"; "But, God, how am I to do that?"). Some people converse with God through journaling or writing their words and then the words of Jesus or God in a dialogical format. When using the written format, the person allows the words of Jesus or God and his responses to come spontaneously instead of writing a script. Others converse directly by writing a poem or letter to God and then writing God's response in a letter or poem back to them.

A fifth pathway to prayer is silent presence. In the other pathways, the individual is the agent of prayer; here the agent is God. This is silent prayer in which the person allows God to be present and to look lovingly upon him; God and the person are in loving gaze upon each other. In the intimacy of silence, the person receives God's loving gaze and returns it. This prayer is centered on attention in faith to the presence of God and on resting in God's love.

Prayer is a lifetime endeavor of growing in loving relationship with the "you" of God. At certain times of prayer an individual experiences consolation, a felt sense that he is cooperating with God in his life. In these times of consolation there may be internal struggle, tension, pain, joy, or satisfaction, yet the person has a certain peace that one is participating in the divine relationship. At other times of prayer, a person may be more desolate, living through a felt sense of the absence of God or through one's exclusion of God by living as if one did all things by oneself. Times of desolation may be painful and confusing as one searches for God; they may be times of felt satisfaction or bliss if one is living more from a stance of self-righteousness and personal grandiosity.

The proper pathway may not be easily accessible for a person who does not always know the best path to take or is not ready to encounter God in a particular way. In the desire to pray, "the Spirit helps us in our weakness; for we do not know how to pray as we ought, but that very Spirit intercedes with sighs too deep for words. And God, who searches the heart, knows what is the mind of the Spirit" (Rom. 8:26–27). One learns how to pray by entering prayer through different pathways.

Prayer and Spiritual Companioning

The spiritual companion relationship is itself a pathway of prayer. It is two people listening together for the word of God in the life of the seeker. It is the contemplation of one's experience in the presence of the Divine that enables him (and also the companion) to grow more fully human in the world in which he lives. The prayer of spiritual companioning is a medium for the development of a life of prayer-in-action of the seeker.

The relationship of spiritual companioning is built upon the desire of the seeker to grow in relationship with God in his lived experience. The focus of the relationship is the seeker's lived experiences as shared in his feelings, thoughts, desires, and actions. The goal of the relationship is attentiveness to God. Through the practice of effective listening, the companion walks with the seeker in his journey to become more self-aware of the activity of God in relation to him and to all of creation. She helps him grow in the practice of attending to God in his particular life, in praying always.

If the goal of the seeker is not specifically focused on his prayer life, the companion initiates the reflection on the presence of God in the other's life. After careful listening to the seeker's experiences, the companion gently asks, "Do you think God might be speaking to you through . . . ," or

"How might God be present in these experiences?" At other times, the companion may ask the seeker, "What do you need from God?" The companion, at times, shares what she has noticed in her listening: "As I listen, I wonder if God might be inviting you to trust your intuition?" These questions and reflections are invitations for the seeker to reflect on God in the midst of his life.

The companion's sensitivity to the person's readiness for this reflection in an individual session and in the relationship is important. One who has an extreme fear of God may not be ready to enter into this type of reflection before trust has been established with the companion. The seeker may need to be led in the practice of prayer in a way that lessens the fear of God. The companion may suggest journaling or working the fear into a clay image or talking to God about his earlier life experiences (of abuse, of learned guilt) that have influenced his fear. In the practice of prayer the seeker comes to know himself better and to grow spiritually.

If the goal of the seeker is to grow in prayer, the companion will invite him to share how he prays now and what have been helpful pathways to prayer for him. The companion will want to know his images of God. It is also helpful for the companion to listen for the ways in which the seeker approaches life, for one often goes about prayer in the way in which he approaches life. For example, a person who is a workaholic may be driven in his prayer; a person who is a natural follower may wait for God's lead in prayer. Knowing how the seeker prays and appreciating who God is for him enable the companion to help the person learn how to pray more fruitfully by offering appropriate pathways to prayer.

The experience of the seeker in praying is the "material" of the relationship. What feelings, images, thoughts, and bodily reactions did the seeker experience during prayer? What insights, challenges, and questions did prayer provide? What seems unfinished? In listening, the companion will invite the seeker to explore the meaning of the images, feelings, thoughts, or bodily experiences that hold the most importance for the seeker. She will walk with him in the exploration of the meaning of his insights, challenges, or questions. She will help him discover what is unfinished and what God might be inviting him to deal with.

Through the development of the person's life of prayer, the companion may notice certain patterned responses to prayer that prompt her to suggest the use of different pathways. For example, the companion notices the seeker's pattern of feeling restless and anxious while talking with God. Exploration of the meaning of these feelings is important, for they may tell something of how one perceives God or something about trust. Talking to God about one's feelings would be a suggested prayer pathway. One might also suggest the use of a mantra prayer for a period of time that will help the person center within. In suggesting a path of prayer, the companion is sensitive to the seeker's personality, history, and present reality. She is aware that the seeker enters into the prayer path and, therefore, chooses and affirms how he might pray at this time of his life.

Companioning another on his path of prayer requires that the companion be aware of her present style(s) of prayer and her patterns of prayer at different stages of life. By reflecting on her present style of prayer and her historical prayer patterns, the companion is able to articulate from her experiences the meaningfulness of certain prayer forms and their relationship to her stages of psychological and spiritual development. She begins to perceive the uniqueness of prayer forms for each individual. This awareness sets her free to listen to the seeker, to affirm his prayer form(s), and to assist him to grow; it frees her from applying solely what works for her onto the other.

The companion's personal recognition of her patterns of prayer and her prayer style includes an awareness of her periods of resistance to the encounter with God. From her spiritual growth in prayer, the companion is able to use herself in the relationship by revealing what worked for her in situations similar to those of the seeker.

Conclusion

To "pray always" is to be attentive to meeting God in one's human reality. It is listening for the word of God in all of oneself. It is the lifetime process of discovering the self and growing fully human. It is the building of the relationship between the "I" that is the self and the "you" that is God. For, as Thomas Merton exclaimed, "If I find [God], I will find myself, and if I find my true self, I will find [God]. . . . The only One Who can teach me to find God is [God], Alone. Pray for your own discovery."[1]

Questions for Reflection

1. What pathway do you most frequently use in prayer?

2. What pathway(s) do you find most difficult? Why?

3. In what way(s) does your particular form of prayer relate to your personality?

4. How have your prayer patterns changed or remained the same over time? *Exercise:* draw a long line, and separate it into five- or ten-year divisions of your life. Reflect on each segment of your life in light of your understanding of prayer and your style of prayer at that time. Write your understanding of prayer above the line and your style below the line. Step back and reflect on the total life pattern when you have completed the exercise.

5. Do you think of yourself as one who prays always? What feelings emerge as you think about this instruction from Jesus?

6. What pathways of prayer are familiar to you in addition to those mentioned in this chapter? How are they pathways?

You may want to write a prayer or a letter to God telling God about your prayer pattern. Or you may wish to use a mantra as you focus on your own prayer line.

chapter 5

Images of God

The history of our ancestors recounts God's instructing Moses to tell his experiences of God to the Israelites: "You have seen what I did to the Egyptians, and how I bore you on eagles' wings and brought you to myself" (Exod. 19:4). Speaking of the realm of God, Jesus described God to be like a sower and like a woman hiding yeast in flour for leavening (Matt. 13:31, 33). Paul proclaimed that Jesus the Christ "is the image of God" (2 Cor. 4:4). Jesus said of himself, "I am the way, and the truth, and the life" (John 14:6).

Experience is communicated sometimes through symbolic language. There is no other way to describe the experience. Reciprocally, images condition experience. The concepts persons have of themselves are derived from their experiences and affect how they relate to and interact with the world and the attitudes with which they encounter God. The images that individuals have of God are also derived from personal and communal experiences and affect their self-perception and their style of relating with others and with God. Images are symbolic representations of personal self-identity and of God identity, who one is and who God is. As symbols, images limit the full expression of the self and of God. The human person is more than any conceptual identity derived from experience; God is more than any metaphor or collection of metaphors used to describe the experience of God.

Images of God and of the self are interrelated; the concepts of the self impact individuals' concept of God and vice versa. As persons' images of God expand, their self-concept becomes stronger, more realistic, and more secure. Psychological development and spiritual growth are complementary functions in the life of the human being. One's image of God, therefore, is a major element in one's view of the world, of others, and of the self that influences the span of one's whole life. The spiritual companion must attend to how a person experiences God within his context and guide him to heal troublesome images of God and to incorporate and expand his God-language relevant to his own experiences.

Parental Experiences

Self-images are constructed early in life primarily through one's relationship with parents and extended family interactions. These early concepts are later reinforced or changed by persons' experiences of others, including their cultural and religious system experiences. Children receive messages of worth or nonworth, of being lovable or unlovable, of belonging or not belonging from the manner in which they are treated by their external world of parental authority. These messages are both overt in the direct parental actions and covert through the words and metaphors children hear about themselves and about the world.

For example, children, who hear constantly "Get out of my way," develop a self-identity as persons who are bothers or who are not welcome in others' lives. Children, who are taught that "You are important to us" by being asked their opinion in family matters, learn that their experiences and feelings are valuable and make a difference. They learn that they are valuable.

The self that individuals learn about in their developing years includes an understanding of their relation to persons in position of authority by virtue of the relationship (parents relating to children). The persons also learn about the place of personal authority in life, the respect given to the self as the author of what is experienced.

Parental authority that is primarily controlling—"Just do what I say; don't question me"—teaches children that they have no rights and that they exist to please authority. These children learn that their experience does not count; they have no authority. Parents who are physically, sexually, or emotionally abusive pass on the message that children are powerless. Children learn that they exist in a world that is domineering and in which they serve as objects of power or as competitive partners for loving relationships.

In contrast, parental authority that embraces children in appropriate love, allowing children to experiment with personal freedom and personal self-discovery, teaches that the self has its own authorship of experience. Children who are asked to share their stories (of school, of playing, of their hurts and joys) grow in viewing the self as respected and cared for as unique persons. They learn that they have power; they have the ability and capacity to influence others. Adults who do not assume appropriate parental authority teach children that they are the center of the universe; there are no rules, social responsibilities, or boundaries in life. Children learn that life is basically nonrelational.

The basic strength, quality, and importance of the self derived from one's childhood directly impacts the individual's concept of God. It is through parental and other adult experiences that the person discovers initially who God is. God is imaged as all-powerful, domineering, loving, receptive, caring, all-knowing, or controlling as the child draws on familial (extended family included) experiences to come to know God.

Individuals formulate how they are to relate to this God based on the quality of their self-image. They see themselves as personally good or bad, adequate or inadequate, worthy or unworthy. Their experiences have taught them to be survivors, partners, objects, powerful, or powerless in relating with peers, with authority, and with God. Persons with a very strong self-identity, such as being the center of the universe, may distort the self as god; whereas persons with a weak self-concept may fear approaching God because of an artificial (unrealistic) personally felt inadequacy.

Social and Cultural Experiences

The social construct of culture (the infrastructure) affects persons' self-identity and their interpretation of God. European-influenced North American culture with its drive toward individualism enculturates persons to view themselves as independent. "Do it on your own" is the message. The European American culture values person-to-object social identity in which emphasis is often placed on knowing a person in terms of status, roles, occupation, and achievements. This culture sets a high priority on hierarchy with its tendency to think and act from an "either-or" or "win-lose" perspective. The self is known as separate from the family or group within the culture with whom one associates. Within the European American culture male experience and authority are honored more than female; heterosexual lifestyles are affirmed more readily than homosexual relationships; power to control is more prevalent than power that empowers persons and a people. European American society in its organization around separate identity deals with authority and power not in terms of relationship but in terms of competition.

African, African American, and Hispanic cultures emphasize and value a person-to-person approach in their social identity. Relationship, an encounter with another, is given prime importance within these cultures. Individual self-identity is of lesser importance than primary and extended familial identity. Asians, Asian Americans, and Native Americans develop and learn about themselves primarily as persons within a group and within a totality of environmental forces. These cultures view themselves as part of a collective identity that includes connection with all of creation. Social identity is less personalized and more community oriented. The self is known through the influences of family and of created nature. The self grows and interacts through person-to-person and person-to-object relationships.[1]

In these cultures women are viewed as keeping the culture together while men are given the authority to regulate and be in charge. Bearing children for the continuation of the culture is very important. The acts of one member in accordance with or dissenting from cultural norms are representative of the group and are addressed within the group. Persons of the African, African American, Hispanic, Asian, Asian American, and Native American cultures care for one another and develop through intrasocial connectedness. These cultures maintain a value of respect for and deference toward elders; reverence of superiors by inferiors is inherent in the way society is organized. Many person-to-person and person-to-group cultures sustain connection with their ancestors; those who have gone before are honored, are sought for advice, and are considered intercessors.

Cultural influences upon individuals vary depending on their gender, sexual orientation, age, and economic status. Experience varies not only within one's own culture but also between cultures. The realities of racism, sexism, classism, and ageism within North American culture create varied (and often conflictual) experiences between one's cultural group and the "cultural norm" of the dominant culture. Persons can learn within the family ethic that they are valued and belong yet are taught by the larger societal culture that they are of no value and are to be excluded. They may learn that mutuality and connectedness are a primary social reality yet be confronted with the message to be self-reliant and self-sufficient. Women (white and of color) may experience acceptance among other women yet feel resistance to their belonging when they assume authority and leadership in a male-dominated culture.

Cultural experiences add to the images of the self and of God acquired through parental experiences. As individuals develop in their interpersonal relationships, cultural influences reinforce their images or introduce conflict and challenges to persons' self-identity and awareness of God. These experiences can enhance and challenge both the negative and the positive images of early childhood.

God may be imaged as similar to the cultural norm or may be experienced as the One who makes up for what is lacking in human experience. For example, a person taught that one is to be self-sufficient may image God as One who is unavailable and distant, the Almighty Other. God, for this person, may also be the only Caring One, the Reliable One. Experiencing exclusion within society, a person may come to know God as the All-Inclusive One who saves or the Almighty Demanding Judge. Learning that one is connected to all of creation, an individual may image God as the Womb of Creation or Universal Energy. One speaks of God as Everlasting, Sustainable Presence.

Religious Experiences

Religious experiences "happen" in different settings. One has a sense of awe in seeing a sunset, an autumn filled with colorful leaves, a winter snowfall. Breaking bread with a homeless person, one experiences eucharist, or receiving the gift of another's time, one feels the love of God. God is experienced in the poor person who gives a quarter to help another; the parable of the widow's mite is reenacted in one's personal reality.

Religious experiences occur in the setting of organized religion. Through the church's functions of teaching, preaching, acting, and ritual life, Christians come to know the reality of basic themes within their lived experiences. Central motifs of Christianity are creation, covenant, incarnation, discipleship, and resurrection.[2] Judeo-Christian belief holds that all persons are created in God's image, are in relationship with God through God's covenant love, and are to be a covenanting people in love with others. Christians profess that God became human in Jesus, that people are called to discipleship and are promised new life. Christians learn about God in themselves and others, about community (covenant), about God through Jesus, about their worth as followers of Jesus in community (discipleship), and about the promise of new life for them individually and collectively from their experiences of church.

Christians learn about God through the church's teaching and preaching of scripture. Images of God in the Hebrew Scriptures are plentiful. God is experienced as light, shadow, fire, water, breath of life, a gentle breeze, and an earthquake. God is named Wisdom, Judge, Warrior, and Holy.[3] The Christian Scriptures recount multiple images of God through the parables of Jesus, stories about Jesus' experience of God. God is like the shepherd looking for the lost sheep and like a woman searching for a lost coin. Jesus proclaims that he is the way, the truth, and the life. Jesus is the Child of God and also Wisdom and Reconciler.[4]

The God of Jesus is a saving, liberating God. The images of God in the Scriptures are embodied in male, female, and nature language. The multiplicity of metaphors for God exemplifies that God is always more than an image. God cannot be limited by image. God is like a shepherd and more than a shepherd. God is Father (Mother) and more than Father (Mother). God is a woman searching for a lost coin and more than such a woman. No one metaphor (or collection of metaphors) of experience adequately names God.

The breadth of the church's teaching and preaching of the images of God limits or expands Christians' awareness of God and their self-image created in God's images. Persons who experience church as noninclusive in the use of scriptural images may be led to discount or count their own experiences as revelatory of God. For example, the exclusive use of male metaphors does not speak to women's experience or to the feminine side of male experiences. Use of all feminine images ignores the importance of women's masculine characteristics and discounts male experiences.

Exclusiveness in the language used to describe God not only constrains the breadth of human reality, but also places boundaries and limits on who God is. A church that limits its images places the community in a position of creating God in its own image and likeness. God is placed in a metaphorical box made in the image and likeness of those who put God there. Experiences of a church that is inclusive and balances the use of scriptural images in its teaching and preaching empower the community to grow in self-other-God identity. As persons' images of God expand, their self-identity and actions become more holistic and vice versa. The opposite is also true. The more limiting of God's images, the more limiting of self-identity and actions.

Church structures and ritual life impact not only one's image of God but also one's lived experience of covenant and discipleship. Persons whose voices and actions are excluded by virtue of ethnicity, race, gender, sexuality, or mental capacity learn that they are not welcome. There is no covenant made with them as they are. These people learn that who they are is not acceptable in the discipleship of Jesus as lived out in the life of the church. They might learn that discipleship is for a few and not for the many. They perceive that the self, known through personal gifts and talents, is outside the fold of Jesus' followers.

For example, the Hispanic or African American members of a predominantly European American congregation are never consulted about liturgical music, or those challenged with mental illness are not welcome on church committees. Other examples are women being excluded from male-dominated church hierarchical structures and devotional rituals that are structurally inflexible to allow for diversity among the congregational members. Those who experience being included within the church according to one's gifts are continually renewed as covenanted people. The more one feels accepted, the greater is one's sense of value and worth, and the more interactive one becomes in creating a dynamic community. As this happens, people feel more included in the process of ongoing creation of the reign of God in the here and now.

Family of origin, society and culture, and church form a triad of human experiences that shape a person's perception of self and of God. They are the underpinnings of how one is in the world and how one relates to God. No one component of this experiential triad is perfect or inclusive. Nor are they together perfect. All are limited. While many have positive experiences from which they live and grow, other experiences wound individuals by forming negative and untrue identity perceptions of self and of God.

Expanding Images

As persons mature and engage in life, they evaluate the images given to them by the outside forces of a particular family, society, and church. As individuals begin to reverence themselves and to give credence to their experiences as unique creatures, they assess their personal experience with what has been previously adopted. Engagement in life confronts individuals with new worldviews and with new views of the self as persons. Persons discover that what is known may be a true reality yet is not the whole reality of their lives in relation to self, to others, and to God. New experiences jar their views, values, and behaviors.

What has been named and claimed by persons at one period in life is no longer applicable in light of their more expanded self-knowledge and knowledge of the broader society in which they live. New experiences (both of the self and of society) call into question the ideologies by which persons have understood the world, themselves, and God. The limitations of the language used to describe experience is apparent, and more expansive language is needed to adequately describe experience. Former images and concepts of the world and of God are either rejected or enhanced by new and more inclusive ones. Psychological development and spiritual growth involve the ongoing process of imaging and reimaging self, others, and God in and through one's lived reality. A Christian's image of God changes as that person changes.

Although life presents many situations that enable a person to grow spiritually, the key to growing through these experiences is the individual's openness to allowing experiences to affect one emotionally and cognitively. One must feel the dissonance between the present experience and one's conceptual models. Feeling the dissonance, a person comes to new understandings and expanded worldviews by allowing the feelings to transform present understandings and worldviews. A person closed to experiences—by choice of involvement or by choice of emotional blocking/denial—stunts personal spiritual growth (and communal growth by association). This openness to life's contradictions is not automatic and comes through experiences of being valued and reverenced as a person of worth and dignity, of being loved for oneself and having one's experiences validated.

To change one's metaphors, one has to engage in a dialogue between what is known and what is newly presented through experience. The Christian's openness to personal experience and to the congruity or discongruity, the completeness or incompleteness of one's images of God sets the stage for greater spiritual maturity. A Christian's openness makes room for the breaking through of God to be revealed in a new way in one's lived reality.

John, a European American male, conditioned to view himself as able to control life, realizes that he cannot control the outcome of the company. *If I cannot control, what good am I?* John thinks. Martha, a woman healing from a history of paternal sexual abuse, is awakened to the fact that God as Father is repulsive to her. "Is God only Father?" she asks. Maurice, an Asian man living in North American culture, experiences racism within his church. "If God is the community of people, then is God selective?" Maurice wonders. Katrina, a woman who thought of herself as weak and unintelligent, earns a master's degree. From this experience, Katrina begins to explore whether she can be woman and intelligent. Margaret, who knows herself as good and lovable, becomes aware of her ability to sin. For the first time, Margaret explores the possibility of her being a sinner and a good person. Until now she thought that a person was either good or sinful.

Situations that call into question a person's conceptual frame of reference are unique to each individual. A contradiction for one person may not be a contradiction or challenge for another. Situations call into question different things for different people. Chronic or acute illnesses, a diagnosis of HIV/AIDS, sobriety from alcohol or drugs, abuse and healing of abuse, death of a loved one or other major loss(es), life's transitions, are examples of some personal crisis situations through which individuals grow in how they see themselves and God. Other times of crisis, as the examples illustrate, are those in which one's self-awareness is enhanced or one is engaged in cultural differences or discriminatory environments.

Spiritual Companioning

The spiritual companion serves as the seeker's Christian guide for the healing of painful/problematic images and for the expansion of new images of God. To be an effective guide, the companion sets aside any of her assumptions and generalizations and attends to the role and importance of the seeker's religious and personal imagery. Aware of the background and culture of the seeker, the companion respectfully listens to his interpretative framework at this time of his life. The companion refrains from promoting one image of God over another or negating an image out of her history. The companion draws on her understanding and expressions of God yet does not force or manipulate the seeker to embody them for himself. The companion honors and respects the seeker's experience, enabling him to name and claim his own experience as the experience of the living God.

In listening to the seeker's experience, the companion attends to the life-giving force of the person's images and to the correlation of his images with his experience. Listening to a seeker's attempt to relate to an "Almighty God" as he struggles with his self-worth in regard to issues of control, the companion is aware of how this image is blocking him. Although the image of Almighty God has served the seeker well in the past, his understanding of God as almighty is not life-giving at this time. Aware that God might be revealing a new meaning for the seeker of God as almighty, the companion suggests that he dialogue with Almighty God in prayer.

At another time, the companion may choose to invite the seeker to explore scripture to find a situation similar to his own. She may also invite him to share what kind of God he needs at this time (God of understanding, God of compassion, God of help) or who he experiences God to be. The companion then suggests that the seeker ask in prayer for God to be present with him. The companion is as unaware as the seeker of the path through which God is to be revealed at this time. Therefore, any one of these paths is appropriate and is used at different times within the relationship as the seeker grows more and more through his experience. God will do God's work.

The spiritual companion is a participant with the seeker in the healing of God images that have been painful for him. A seeker wounded emotionally by maternal abuse has lived with the absence of motherly care yet has learned that God is Compassionate One. In speaking of his image of God as compassion, the seeker shares that this God is utterly impossible for him to relate to. Yet this image is very important to him because he believes firmly that the world needs compassion and that he is called to be compassionate.

The companion is aware of the seeker's need to be healed of the wounds of his image and to maintain the image. Healing of images always requires a letting go of the meaning of the problematic images and giving birth to new images. Yet it does not always mean permanently discarding the image. To guide the seeker in the letting go of the image, the companion enters into the process of dealing with the loss of one's symbolic system. She asks the seeker to express (orally, in clay, poetry, journaling) what the image has meant, what it would mean for the seeker to let go of it, what he would give up and what he would gain by either keeping the image or letting it go.

The companion searches over time with the seeker what will be liberating for him. As the choice for liberation is discovered, the companion then guides the seeker to let go of the problematic image at this period of his life. She inquires how he thinks or feels he can best let go of the image. What God does he need to help him to this, or to be with him, or to celebrate with him? The companion guides the seeker then to call upon that God, to reimage God in this new way before he lets go of the Compassionate One. After several sessions (or months), the seeker may be ready to reincorporate the Compassionate One into his life along with the new image. Often the seeker makes this known through his use of language and what he presents in a session. The companion is to wait and to listen.

The spiritual companion partners with the seeker in opening up the multiplicity of human awareness of God from her experience of scripture, the life of others, her spiritual journey and, in particular, his experiences. In listening to the life story of the seeker, the companion attends to the connection of his self-images and his images of God and to how these images are related to the Judeo-Christian biblical themes. She is cognizant of how the seeker images God and assists him in naming God.

Asking the seeker early on to share how he images God gives the companion a foundational knowledge of the seeker that is imperative to the purpose of the relationship. She may offer some broad suggestions to help the neophyte in naming his experience. "Is God like a mother, a father, an uncle, a tree, a lamb, a waterfall?" Throughout the relationship, the companion occasionally asks the seeker, "Who is God for you today [in this experience, in your fearing, in your joy]?" This enables the seeker to bring to consciousness his own images and the companion to connect the seeker's experience with biblical stories or with experiences of other Christians. The companion affirms the image and, occasionally, adds one that has emerged for her as she listened to the seeker.

At other times of the relationship, the companion offers feedback to the seeker in terms of how she images God present in the life of the seeker. This feedback is done out of her intuition, her familiarity with scriptural images ("It sounds as if God is fire burning within you"), and her connectedness with the seeker's culture and journey. The companion's suggestions for prayer also aid the seeker to expand his language of God as he grows spiritually. Inviting the seeker to use the imagination through art, clay, or other noncognitive ways is very helpful at times. Utilizing a different medium can assist the seeker in expressing and affirming his experiences.

Conclusion

A Christian seeker's images of God affect and are affected by his experience. Spiritual growth involves the ongoing process of attending to and identifying God through experiences. Christians bring to this attending the experiences of God of the past, including those of their biblical ancestors and of Jesus. The more experiences one reflects upon, the more God is truly revealed and the more fully human one becomes. Yet God is always more than experience reveals. God is and God is not contained in the image. The language of imagination cannot fully express God. Ultimately, God is Holy Mystery.

Questions for Reflection

1. What images of God did you learn from your family, your society and culture, the church?

2. What identity of self did you learn from your family, your society and culture, the church?

3. Who is God for you today?

4. What significant events or people helped you to broaden your images of self and of God?

5. What is your favorite biblical passage? What image of God is portrayed? Do you speak to God through that image? In what way does that image connect with your self-image?

6. Read Luke 8:16–18. Allow yourself to enter the image. Be open to new images of God's vision as you allow the passage to speak to you.

You may wish to explore your openness and response to various images of God that are familiar and unfamiliar to you. This can be done several times, each time being focused on only one image. Relax; quiet yourself; be still. Address God with one of the following names and allow that God to be present with you. Enter into whatever the name evokes. Images of God: Fire, Shelter, Breath, Wisdom, Shadow, Mother, Father, Energy, Child, Body, Lover, Friend, Judge, Holy Mystery.

chapter 6

Personality Awareness

No person can be understood totally. Each person's personality is a unique pattern of traits, attitudes, values, actions, thoughts, and feelings. The childhood formation of personality occurs from the constellation of personal history, gifts, weaknesses, strengths, genetics, and consciousness of experiences. Core elements of one's personality are shared with others whose early life experiences are similar; elements are imprinted on the personality resulting from childhood experiences.

As the child grows and develops the cognitive ability of differentiation and selection, the options for choosing from one's experience become greater. The character of the personality becomes more complex and is constructed from a wider scope of options relating to roles, relationships, status, and other direct and indirect influences. Augsburger speaks of a primary personality core and a secondary personality complex.[1] Primary is that of childhood held in common with others; secondary is that of later life. A person's unique personality emerges as one selects from multiple experiential options.

Human development theories and personality typologies are organized around similarities and differences of people. They are tools that help persons affirm themselves and relate more effectively with others. Becoming aware of these theories and typologies, the companion is better able to appreciate the seeker (and herself as well) in how he interacts with the world, God, and himself. She can enter his world more empathically (and interpathically) and walk with him in his holistic growth. The companion avoids the temptation to stereotype or label while drawing on her knowledge in relating with the seeker.

Human Development Theories

The developmental theories of Erik Erikson and Gail Sheehy identify periods within the life cycle as stages or points of passage in which the individual negotiates certain tasks. Beginning with birth, Erikson identifies these periods of the human life cycle: infancy, early childhood, childhood, adolescence, young adulthood, middle adulthood, and maturity.[2] Within each biological period persons are confronted with a relational crisis that they must resolve in their personality development. The degree to which individuals resolve these crises constitutes the strength of their personal development.

The developmental task of each period involves the negotiation of certain relational issues. Erikson identifies these relational issues as trust vs. mistrust, autonomy vs. shame, initiative vs. guilt, industry vs. inferiority, identity vs. role confusion, intimacy vs. isolation, generativity vs. stagnation, and integrity vs. despair. The corresponding virtues associated with each period of development are hope, will, purpose, competence, fidelity, love, care, and wisdom.

Persons must adequately resolve the issues of one period before they can manage those of the next stage. Personal development occurs sequentially, although different life events precipitate persons' reengagement of an earlier developmental issue at a deeper level. Biological growth continues regardless of how well persons perform their developmental tasks; getting older biologically does not equate gaining personal maturity. For example, an individual in his forties may be struggling with early issues of trust and mistrust. Another person in his forties may be dealing with trust and mistrust at a deeper level. The developmental tasks identified by Erikson are applicable to men and women, yet the sequence beginning with autonomy and moving toward intimacy does not coincide with women's developmental patterns.

The works of Carol Gilligan,[3] Jean Baker Miller, and others at the Stone Center[4] demonstrate that women develop the self by beginning with connection and relationship and growing toward separateness and connection. While the young boy learns that he is not like his mother and is generally led to formation of separate identity, the young girl identifies with the mother and grows in connection and identity with the mother. Unlike men who deal with self-identity as separate individuals (autonomy) before facing issues of intimacy, women develop intimacy through identity. Being connected is a key factor in a woman's development as she grows to know her individuated self among others. While these theories balance those of Erikson within the European American community, they do not speak per se to the development of persons of color. As chapter 5 discusses, most African, African American, and Asian men and women develop identities of relation and connection similar to the studies of Gilligan and others.

Gail Sheehy identifies a person's growth as a series of losses and rebirths, a pattern of the death of one self-identity and the emergence of a more mature self.[5] The teen years she envisions as the years of pulling up roots from family and moving into provisional adulthood. The twenties are years of transition, as are the thirties and early forties. From the early twenties through the early forties a person moves from "I should" to "I want" to "I must." Sheehy notes a gradual movement in development from external obedience to internal desire to commitment. The years of the late forties and fifties are viewed as restabilization and flowering, the years of full bloom. The remaining years are life-filled and full of energy and creativity. Life, Sheehy discovered, does not end at fifty; it begins with new vigor.

Lawrence Kohlberg[6] and Mary Belenky and her colleagues[7] describe persons' development in coming to know truth. Kohlberg's stages of moral development center on the evolution of moral reasoning in boys and men based on a framework of rights. From this conception of individual rights, Kohlberg identifies six stages of moral development: punishment and obedience, individual instrumental purpose and exchange, mutual interpersonal expectations, relationship and conformity, social system and conscience maintenance, rights and universal ethical principles. This model of development presupposes that persons have a separate self-identity from which they know the truth and become moral beings. Kohlberg views the self as having individual autonomy who knows and acts through rationality.

Belenky and her colleagues describe the perspectives from which women view reality and come to truth, knowledge, and a sense of authority. Contrary to Kohlberg's concept of individual rights, the moral development of women intersects with their self-concept and struggle to claim personal power. Rather than developing individualistically, women develop relationally. Women's concept of self moves from that of doing what "they say" to an appreciation of themselves in integrating their voices with those of others, in constructing truth and feeling related even in the midst of differences.

Women grow in the process of owning their authority, giving credence to their voices, through the path of received knowledge, subjective knowledge, procedural knowledge, and constructed knowledge. Received knowledge is knowledge originating from outside the self. Listening to the voices of others, women define themselves in terms of social expectations and social/occupational roles. Subjective knowledge is that gained from women's attention to their inner voice and the quest for the self.

At this juncture of development, women become aware of their personal inner resources and begin to identify boundaries in relationships. They discover the intuited self and personal importance, and women feel a sense of liberation from being silent members of society. Women may experience conflict as the self is emerging and new connections with the world are being forged. Watching and listening to the outside world and to their inner world of self, women struggle and grow to honor both themselves and others. Growth in procedural knowledge is that period when women combine the received knowledge and subjective knowledge gained and engage in conscious, deliberate, and systemic analysis. Reasoned reflection using personal knowledge and a desire to understand others' ways of thinking are key procedures in women's gathering of others' knowledge. Women enter into collaboration with others in discovery of what is truth; their voices and those of others are important. Finally, women construct knowledge through collaboration and integration, identifying truth as a matter of the context in which it is embedded. Women maintain their individuality and its versatility within various contexts.

Though Kohlberg formulates his theory from male studies and Belenky and others identify women's ways of knowing, it would be unfair to label all men or all women included or excluded from either representation. As in the models of Erikson and Sheehy, these theories are frames of reference for the spiritual companion as she listens with the seeker. Spiritual growth is interconnected with personal growth; issues in development often parallel issues in one's spiritual development.

Authority: Cultural Development

Inherent in personal development are one's views of personal power or authority. Building relationship includes one's sense of belonging and one's sense of authority, the power to "author" or influence life and others. A seeker's understanding of power is culturally conditioned, affecting his personality and, consequently, his relationships with others and with God. Similarly, the companion's sense of authority impacts how she relates and listens with the seeker. Personal and cultural understandings of authority demand that the companion be attentive and respectful of the Christian's (and her own) power while enabling him to grow spiritually. This integration involves an appropriate balance of power congruent with one's culture and with Christian beliefs. The discernment of self-authority, divine authority, and the messages of Christianity is an important aspect of spiritual growth.

One locus of authority is in the power of control. Individuals identify themselves as controlling life, being controlled by life, or somewhere on a continuum of internal and external control.[8] These views of the self relative to who is in charge of life place value priorities on dependency, interdependency, and independence. Western culture in its more individualistic (and rights-oriented) perspective tends toward an emphasis on internal control; the person controls life. Value is placed on independence, relegating dependency and interdependency as lesser or negative values.

Yet within this culture, members of a middle or lower economic class, women, and racial minorities are enculturated toward external control, and value is placed on their being dependent; societal membership requires dependency. These oppressed members within Western culture can feel a strong sense of helplessness and a loss of appropriate internal control in their lives. A seeker who has learned that dependency is associated with belonging may give the companion power to control him; whereas one with a strong internal control identity may struggle to share with the companion. God could be the external controller in the former situation and the unavailable one in the latter situation. Through her compassionate presence and guidance, the companion fosters a reclaiming of the seeker's power of control and a balancing of internal-external control that is life-giving.

Eastern cultures, for the most part, view the path of social development differently from the way that Western cultures do. Dependence in a group-centered identity is fostered over independence; cultural value is placed on group belonging. Within these cultures, external controls—of family, of systems, of community—upon the members are perceived as good power. Control from the outside is normative within these cultures and is considered necessary for the good of everyone. There are peoples, however, within these cultures for whom control from external sources has become oppressive. Congruent with their group-centered identity, persons of Eastern cultures are more private than those of Western cultures; they tend to observe and listen to others before speaking their thoughts and feelings.

Therefore, a seeker of Eastern heritage may, by virtue of his positive cultural experiences, depend appropriately on the companion for direction in claiming his authority. A seeker having felt overly controlled and oppressed from external authority may relate dependently more out of fear than from cultural norms. While reverencing his privacy, the companion aids the Eastern seeker by accepting the dependency and asking him to share how this is helpful to him. She assists him in being an observer and discerner of his life within a culture unlike his.

Another locus of authority that goes hand in hand with control is the individual's sense of responsibility and accountability. Persons view responsibility for living, achieving, and relating either internally or externally, within themselves or outside themselves in others or in systems. Western cultural norms hold individuals responsible for their lives; credit and blame rest with the individual. Those controlled (oppressed) by Western society are often individually blamed and discredited for their life conditions. These people grow spiritually not only by claiming their inner power to control their lives but also by claiming appropriate responsibility for allowing oppression to affect them. Those living as if everything depended on them grow spiritually in sharing responsibility and control with others.

Many non-Western cultures view responsibility more externally; accountability for living rests within social structures and among peoples. Growth spiritually for those viewing all responsibility outside themselves includes a movement toward self-identified responsibility. Once again, a seeker's (and companion's) concept of responsibility affects how he relates within the spiritual relationship and with God. Attending to the seeker's language as he talks about his experiences, his needs from her, and his images of God, the companion walks with him in Christian authority. Reflection on Jesus' authority within his social context provides the Christian seeker (and companion) concrete guidance for his life. Key questions the companion may raise for the seeker are: What is the locus of Jesus' power? How does Jesus respect the culture of his time, and how does he challenge it? In any one passage of the Christian Scriptures, what is Jesus saying about control and responsibility?

Myers-Briggs Type Indicator

The Myers-Briggs Type Indicator is one of several typologies that function as tools for understanding human personality based on one's orientation toward life. Interfacing with Carl Jung's work, the Myers-Briggs typology is constructed around individuals' (though it is applicable to groups) basic stance in relation to the world and their cognitive and affective processes used in interacting with the world. It provides the companion with a way of appreciating a seeker's uniqueness while giving her guidance for assisting his spiritual development.

Jung discovered that persons have four essential preferences in relating to the world and in processing data they receive from the world.[9] He organized these preferences in four pairs: extraversion (E) and introversion (I), perceiving (P) and judging (J), sensing (S) and intuition (N), feeling (F) and thinking (T).

Extraverts are energized by the outside world and the company of others; introverts prefer the inner world of self and ideas. Perceiving is the process of gathering data and is done through either the physical senses or the inner urgings of intuition. Judging is the processing or prioritizing of the data received and is accomplished through the affective function of feeling or the cognitive function of thinking. All preferences are part of each person's personality and are inherently equal to each other, yet persons enhance one function of each pair over the other as the personality develops.

In light of Jung's model, persons can relate to the world and process the data received from the world in one of sixteen possible preferential patterns known as the Myers-Briggs Type Indicator (MBTI). These patterns are INTJ, INTP, INFJ, INFP, ISTJ, ISTP, ISFJ, ISFP, ENTJ, ENTP, ENFJ, ENFP, ESTJ, ESTP, ESFJ, and ESFP. Persons prefer relating through extraversion (E) or introversion (I) and processing data through functions of perceiving (P) or judging (J).

A person with an INTJ-type personality, for example, is an introvert (I) who prefers to prioritize or draw conclusions (J) about data perceived. Since this person prefers judging to perceiving, her judging function of thinking (T) will be her dominant mode of behavior; her perceiving function of intuition (N) is an auxiliary or helping mode. This person thinks about the information she gathered through her intuition. Because she is an introvert, her thinking occurs within herself, and her intuitive self is the face she shows to the outside world. An INTJ companion approaches her listening through intuition and makes decisions through thinking. An INTJ seeker is experienced as an intuitive person thinking through decisions. Extraversion, sensate ability, and the feeling self are present yet less utilized in one's interactions.

An ENFP type, for example, is an extravert (E) perceiver (P) whose dominant mode is in the perceiving function of intuition (N), which is helped by his auxiliary feeling (F) function. This person gathers data through his intuition and makes decisions about the data based primarily on feelings. Because he is an extravert, his intuitive self is shown outside himself, and his feelings are more within. An ENFP companion approaches the relationship through her intuition and makes judgments based on her feelings. An ENFP seeker is experienced as an intuitive person who judges through feelings. Introversion, thinking ability, and one's senses are available, too, yet less preferred in encounters with others.

According to the MBTI, persons mature through the integration of all eight functions exemplified in Jung's four pairs of preferences. The path of integration develops throughout life as individuals acquire the less preferred or shadow functions of the personality. This integration generally occurs by the growth of the dominant and auxiliary functions first, followed by the opposite of these functions. The opposite of the auxiliary is usually cultivated in the mid years of the forties and fifties, and that of the dominant (considered one's inferior function) is integrated in the postmidlife years. Specific helps in this integration of one's personality related to the spiritual journey are discussed in the following chapter on spiritual development.

Enneagram

Although the origin of the Enneagram is unknown, some credit its development to the Sufi tradition, a mystical Islamic tradition of the Middle Ages. Like other typologies, the Enneagram is a model of human personalities demonstrating that certain groups of people have certain characteristics. Unlike other typologies, the Enneagram describes personality structures of individuals based on particular compulsions and possibilities for change. The central focus of the Enneagram is that of conversion, the invitation to enter into a path of change or "redemption." The foundation of the Enneagram presupposes the person as divinely created, good, and open to the grace of transformation. Individuals' compulsions or "root sin" when claimed by them become gifts and the means of transformative grace. The Enneagram is a tool for persons to claim the healing and redemptive power within them. It is a tool for the discernment of spirits.

The starting point of the Enneagram is the "root sin" or unredeemed compulsions inherent in individuals' personalities. These compulsions are developed from early childhood and are the behavioral patterns persons used in adapting to or in surviving their environment. Persons' unredeemed compulsions are their defensive positions that protect the self against feelings of elemental fear.

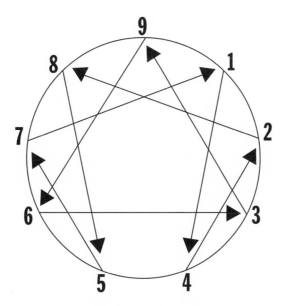

Figure 1. THE ENNEAGRAM

The Enneagram tradition perceives that persons develop one of nine ("enneas") basic profiles by which individuals face the world from their compulsions and defenses (see figure 1). These patterns are represented by a circle numbered clockwise from one through nine. Profiles 3, 6, and 9 are connected by an equilateral triangle, and a hexagon of arrows connects points 1, 4, 2, 8, 5, and 7. The circle visualizes the inclusion of the characteristics of all nine profiles within each person, the profiles that are "redeeming," and the profiles that one tends to adapt when stressed (indicated by arrows toward and away from each number). The latter profiles create a disintegration of the self-identity into greater compulsion.

The compulsions associated with each number correspond to who one thinks one is or needs to be. Persons see themselves as hardworking (1), helpful (2), successful (3), unique (4), all-knowing (5), loyal (6), nice (7), powerful (8), or okay (9). The corresponding threats to be avoided and against which persons developed their defenses are anger, neediness, failure, ordinariness, emptiness, deviance, pain, weakness, and conflict. The positive attitudes or gifts contained within each profile are those of honesty (1), assistance (2), administration (3), creativity (4), wisdom (5), facilitation (6), optimism (7), advocacy (8), and the gift of negotiation (9).

Individuals' spiritual growth resides in claiming their compulsions and gifts (their basic selves) and moving toward healing in incorporating the characteristics of their "redeemed" profile as well as those of other profiles. Integration moves toward healing and giftedness and away from compulsion. For example, an unredeemed One perceives the self as hardworking and acts from a need to be perfect while defending against anger. The One moves toward healing by integrating the characteristics of a Seven and tends toward ("disintegrates") the characteristics of a Four in stress. An unredeemed Four integrates the identity of a One in healing and adopts the compulsions of a Two when stressed.[10]

Karen Horney identified three ways persons overcome their inherent fear in relating to others. Following her work, the Enneagram names three body centers from which individuals relate. Those relating from a gut center (Types 8, 9, 1) tend to relate instinctively and are unconsciously or consciously governed by aggression against others (Horney's hostility), demanding their own space and justice for others. Persons relating more from a well-defined sense of responsibility and a concern for being with others (Types 2, 3, 4) are heart-centered (Horney's submission or directed types). Types 5, 6, 7, head-centered, are drawn away from others (Horney's isolation), thinking things through and acting methodically while hiding their feelings from others. Gut-centered people appear self-confident and strong while inwardly experiencing doubts. Heart-centered individuals appear self-confident and happy while feeling inadequate and shameful. Head-centered people face the world as clear-minded and convincing yet inwardly struggle with feelings of confusion and meaninglessness. Ways of using the personality profiles of the Enneagram in assisting the healing and redemptive power of the seeker are discussed in the following chapter.[11]

Conclusion

An individual's personality is the ground for spirituality. How persons understand themselves and others and identify their ways of relating in the world directly correlates with their relationship with God. Understanding and appreciating a person's personality from a Christian perspective are based on two basic truths. First, the personality of each person is always more than is revealed through consciousness; a person is more than what is known. Second, a person's personality is the medium through which God reveals God's self and through which a person grows toward wholeness.

The companion in using the tools of personality theories and typologies enters into the life of the seeker more empathically (and interpathically) in appreciating her own gifts and limits and those of the seeker. The companion relationship is enriched by the companion's awareness of personality development and her attentiveness to the issues and concerns of the seeker.

Questions for Reflection

1. At what stage of development are you? What issues are you dealing with?
2. What has been your way of knowing truth?

3. How do you view your personal power or authority? What role do external control and responsibility play in relation to internal control and responsibility? How do you understand God's authority and power in relation to you?

4. Would you identify yourself as a Perceiver or Judger? Thinker or Feeler? Extravert or Introvert? Sensate or Intuitive? How does your personality profile affect how you listen and how you pray?

5. What is your compulsion? What undeveloped personality characteristics are becoming more available to you in your spiritual path?

6. What type of personality "rubs" you the wrong way? Are you willing to talk to God about this personality in yourself? Will you?

After reflecting on these questions, you are invited to enter into prayer utilizing an adaptation of a form of prayer called haiku. This form of prayer is based on tapping in to your consciousness and connecting an external reality with the Word of God within you. The adaptation involves your writing a five-line poem given specific directions and then reading and pondering the "voice" of the poem spoken to you.

Here are guides for writing your poem. First line: write a noun—any noun that comes to you. Second line: write an adjective that describes your noun. Third line: write a phrase of five or more words that tells more about your described noun. Fourth line: write down a request of God. Fifth line: write God's response to you. Now, slowly read and ponder your poem. What is the message for you as a companion?

As an example, one person's poem became:

Sky
Overhead
Blue, gray, cloudy, full, and empty at times
Are you there, God
Yes

chapter 7

Being Transformed in
God by God

Christian spiritual development is a lifelong process of being transformed in God by God. It is a transformation of the whole human personality toward the highest possible degree of living in the spirit of Jesus, a spirit of fidelity to the reign of God and to God. Efficacious spiritual development moves human reality in the direction of the reign of God and in closer union with God. Spiritual growth is, ultimately, the movement toward a life of surrender to love, to God's way, in one's moment of sacred history.

The Judeo-Christian story is a dialogue between God, the Initiator, and God's people; it is a dialogue spoken in deeds and words by both God and God's people. The story recounts how the Word of God requires a response from believers who undergo a metanoia or interior change in their covenanted life with God. In the incarnation the fullness of God in human reality became manifest in Jesus (Col. 1:19). Based on life in Jesus, Christian spiritual development demands that individuals, whom God has called by name (Isa. 43:1), hear the Word of God through Jesus in their existential lives and perceive what God requires of them in bringing about the reign of God. Hearing and perceiving, the Christian believer responds in word and deed and is changed in becoming more fully human, created in God's image.

For the Christian, spiritual growth is possible through all of human reality. The providential God is a God of all possibility who cooperates with humanity to bring all things—hatred, oppression, revenge, ostracization—into good through Jesus. "You did not choose me but I chose you . . . that you may love one another" (John 15:16–17). Nothing "will be able to separate us from the love of God in Christ Jesus" (Rom. 8:39). Spiritual development is truly an approach to the mystery of God.

Views of the Path of Spiritual Development

Christianity has a rich history of the paths of spiritual development. Many of the earlier spiritual traditions are based on a dualistic worldview in which the spiritual life is considered outside the realm of reality. Spiritual growth was equated with climbing to the mountaintop, going into the desert to find God, or denouncing all worldly things. The flesh was seen as negative and an evil to be overcome. Spirituality was viewed as an individualistic occurrence to be accomplished in the solitude of meditation, retreat, and personal conversion. Christian spirituality in its best sense is "mysticism," the experience of the Spirit, yet relates today with God's intimate communication with humanity in and through Jesus, the Word made flesh. Contemporary Christian spirituality remembers the past while being totally immersed in the creation of a just and God-centered human existence. It is relational development based on the truths of Christianity.

Using the richness of the mystical tradition, Carol Ochs reinterprets the stages of mysticism based on a concept of the spiritual life as a walk during which the Christian observes and interprets one's surroundings and experiences.[1] The stages of mysticism used by Ochs are awakening, purgation, illumination, dark night of the soul, and unitive life. Individuals are awakened to reality being larger than oneself and are transformed by the realization that meaning is determined not by the self but by something outside the self. This awakening, Ochs maintains, is repetitive as persons first forget their relatedness and then experience a renewed awareness of being more than oneself. The awakened self is transformed to express a permanent way of life that seeks to rid oneself (purgation) of blocks to relationships; tasks are done out of love rather than duty.

Having been transformed toward loving relationships, individuals have periods of illumination, of new visions of the world in its beauty and splendor, and periods of pain and trials when all seems to go wrong. These latter periods of darkness Ochs identifies as the times when individuals struggle to let go of aspects of love that are primarily self-centered. The unitive life is always present as God is always present. Viewed in this perspective, spiritual growth is a series of losing connection, recovering it, forgetting it, and rediscovering it.

Francis Nemeck and Marie Coombs perceive human spiritual development as one aspect of the genesis or the becoming more and more in God.[2] All of creation and each creature within creation is moving in a spiritual direction into the Divine. Every human creature according to one's personality, life events, and circumstances has a unique spiritual direction into the Divine. In the course of one's spiritual direction there are periods of divine breakthrough in which the individual discards and/or realigns one's values and priorities and chooses a new mode of being in life. As each of these new "thresholds" or spiritual awakenings of the spiritual life is engaged, the Spirit continues to lead one to an even deeper quality of life in Christ; individuals feel at home in a new life in God and then experience a renewed restlessness with a sense that there is more.

The Spirit leads one in a rhythm of immersion in creation for Christ and emergence through creation with Christ. The believer immerses in creation, becoming more aware of God and of Christ, and emerges with an ever increasing positive quality in living for the self and for others because of God and Christ. Immersion is more than engagement; it is reflected engagement informed by faith in God present in human reality. The Ignatian Exercises and the Interior Castles of St. Teresa of Jesus are traditional ways that assist one through the paths of immersion and decision making in choosing how one is going to live.

From a life of immersion-emergence a person moves to the threshold of personal conversion, a desire to surrender oneself wholeheartedly to God through Jesus in love, hope, and faith. Radical abandonment, an insatiable yearning for union with the Divine, is an intensification of this personal conversion. Spiritual development of the human person, from individual creation in birth through personal death, is an individual's continuous creation into the fullness of God's image through divine-human cooperation.

Henri Nouwen in *Reaching Out* identifies spiritual growth as sequential movements: reaching out to one's inner self, reaching out to other human beings, and reaching out to God.[3] The Christian's path is a movement from loneliness to solitude, from hostility to hospitality, from illusion to prayer. In the first movement a person grows from feeling alone and disconnected to experiencing the inner self as a place of quiet creativity. The second movement is the transformation from keeping others out to reaching out to others in hospitality and welcome. The third movement in spiritual growth is the reaching out to God from the heart and away from false or delusional images of God unrelated to human history and personal experiences.

Spiritual Development through Personality Typologies

An understanding of human personality through the Myers-Briggs and the Enneagram is helpful in transforming one's personality through integration and balance. The Center for Application of Psychological Type charts outline the spiritual paths associated with the Myers-Briggs personality function.[4] "Finding Your Spiritual Path" (figure 2) illustrates how each preference shapes various areas of one's spiritual path and identifies the dynamics for each preference in nurturing the less preferred function. For example, extraverts' primary arena is the outer world with a preference for action. Extraverts are more comfortable with corporate prayer, and their natural spiritual path is through action; whereas introverts' natural path is through reflection. The need for wholeness for extraverts is reflection, and for introverts the need is for participation.

"Following Your Spiritual Path" (figure 3) illustrates the dynamics involved in integrating the less preferred ways (the shadow side) of relating to the world and processing data that help persons become more fully human in their discovery of God. It transposes the needs for wholeness and offers

Figure 2. Finding Your Spiritual Path

Note: These words are meant to suggest, not to define or to limit understanding.

PREFERRED ATTITUDE, FUNCTION OR LIFESTYLE	EXTRAVERSION E	INTROVERSION I	SENSING S	INTUITION N	THINKING T	FEELING F	JUDGMENT J	PERCEPTION P
PRIMARY ARENA	WORLD/OTHER	IDEAS/SELF	BODY	SPIRIT	MIND	HEART	WILL	AWARENESS
PREFERENCE FOR	Action	Reflection	Sensory reality Details Status Quo	Possibilities Patterns Change	Objective values	Subjective values	Initiative	Response
SIGNIFICANT ASPECTS OF REALITY	Exterior	Interior	Immediacy Concreteness	Anticipation Vision	Theory Principles	Feeling Memory Ideal	Product Categorical	Process Conditional
WINDOWS THROUGH WHICH GOD'S REVELATION IS RECEIVED	People Events Scripture Natural world	Individual experience Inspiration Inner world	Society Institutions "The Seen"	Insight Imagination "The Unseen"	Reason Speculation	Relationships Emotions	Order "Ought"	Serendipity "Is"
SIGNIFICANT ASPECTS OF GOD	Immanence Creator Imago Dei	Transcendence Identity of God and inner self	Incarnation	Mystery Holy Spirit	The Absolute Principle First Cause	Relational Familial (e.g. Father)	Judge Ruler	Redeemer Healer
APPROACH TO BIBLE, RELIGIOUS EXPERIENCE	Social	Solitary	Practical Literal	Symbolic Metaphorical	Analytical Abstract	Personal Immediate	Systematic	Of-the-moment
AVOIDS (HELL)	Exclusion Loneliness	Intrusions Confusion	Ambiguity	Restriction Repetition	Inconsistency Ignorance	Conflict Estrangement	Helplessness Disorder	Regimentation Deadlines
SEEKS (HEAVEN)	Participation Reunion	Incorporation Fulfillment	Physical harmony Faithfulness Obedience	Aesthetic harmony Mystical union	Conceptual harmony Enlightenment Justice, Truth	Personal harmony Communion Appreciation	Closure Productivity Work ethic	Openness Receptivity Play ethic
PRAYER	Corporate	Private	Sensuous (eyes, ears, nose, hands, mouth)	Intuitive	Cognitive	Affective	Planned	Unplanned
NATURAL SPIRITUAL PATH	ACTION	REFLECTION	SERVICE	AWARENESS	KNOWLEDGE	DEVOTION	DISCIPLINE	SPONTANEITY
NEEDED FOR WHOLENESS	Reflection	Action or Participation	Awareness or Understanding	Service or Embodiment	Devotion	Knowledge	Spontaneity	Discipline

Published by Center for Applications of Psychological Type, Inc., 2815 N.W. 13th Street, Suite 401 • Gainesville, Florida 32609-2816 • Toll free 800 777-2278. Developed by Earle C. Page. Copyright 1982 CAPT • Duplication or storage of this form, by any means, is strictly prohibited. CAPT, the CAPT logo, and Center for Applications of Psychological Type are trademarks of Center for Applications of Psychological Type, Inc., Gainesville, FL. Used with permission.

Figure 3. FOLLOWING YOUR SPIRITUAL PATH

Note: Our aim is a balanced, centered spirituality. These words are meant to facilitate understanding, not to stifle individuality.

SPIRITUAL PATH	ACTION E	REFLECTION I	SERVICE S	AWARENESS N	KNOWLEDGE T	DEVOTION F	DISCIPLINE J	SPONTANEITY P
SOME POSITIVE EXPRESSIONS	Assertiveness Building community	Independence Deepening community	Love Pleasure	Ecstasy Anticipation	Equanimity Objectivity	Compassion Rapport Trust	Discrimination Competence	Acceptance Serenity
SOME NEGATIVE EXPRESSIONS	Anger Attack	Fear Withdrawal	Attachment	Elation Depression	Apathy Criticalness	Sentimentality Over-protectiveness	Inappropriate control Judging others	Failure to take responsibility
UNDER-DEVELOPMENT MAY LEAD TO	Isolation Lack of circumspection	Emptiness Dependence	Abstraction Overlooking	Flatness	Confusion	Coldness Distrust	Loss of purpose Indecision	Premature closure Baseless conclusions
OVER-DEVELOPMENT MAY LEAD TO	Impatience Shallowness	Withholding Idiosyncrasy Inappropriate intensity	Idolatry Frivolity Inappropriate conformity	Illusion Impracticality Stubbornness Fickleness	Reductionism Cynicism Dogmatism Rumination	Credulity Personalizing Blaming	Rigidity Perfectionism	Passivity Impulsiveness Procrastination
SPECIAL TEMPTATIONS AND VULNERABILITIES	Distraction Suggestibility	Inaction Inclusion by others	Superstition Suspicion Fear of change	Primitive sensuality Psychogenic illness	Emotional explosion, exploitation, indulgence Contaminated thinking	Idealizing authority Pseudo-objectivity Hurt feelings	Self-righteousness Scrupulosity	Rebelliousness Carelessness
NEEDED FOR WHOLENESS	REFLECTION	ACTION or Participation	AWARENESS	SERVICE or Embodiment	DEVOTION	KNOWLEDGE	SPONTANEITY	DISCIPLINE

Finding Your Spiritual Path and *Following Your Spiritual Path* were developed to help individuals and groups use C. G. Jung's observations about psychological type as a way to find their individual and group journeys toward wholeness. The words and phrases are meant to open you to new aspects of this search.

Published by Center for Applications of Psychological Type, Inc., 2815 N.W. 13th Street, Suite 401 • Gainesville, Florida 32609-2816 • Toll free 800 777-2278. Developed by Earle C. Page. Copyright 1982 CAPT • Duplication or storage of this form, by any means, is strictly prohibited. CAPT, the CAPT logo, and Center for Applications of Psychological Type are trademarks of Center for Applications of Psychological Type, Inc., Gainesville, FL. Used with permission.

insight into positive and negative expressions of each preference, identifies the pitfalls of underdevelopment or overdevelopment of one's preference, and lists special temptations and vulnerabilities associated with each preference. For example, assertiveness is a positive expression for extraverts, and anger or attack is a form of negative expression. Underdeveloped extraversion leads to isolation, and overdevelopment leads to impatience and shallowness. The special temptation for extraverts is distractions, and they are vulnerable to suggestions from others.

The Enneagram path is perceived as the transformation of one's compulsion ("root sin") to gifts in integrating the less developed aspects of the personality. The goal of the path is to meet the face of God in all of oneself and in others unlike the self. Spiritual conversion is a matter of recognizing and claiming what stirs the inner self (one's Type), identifying when one's characteristics lead to destructive and constructive behaviors (barriers and grace), and being transformed through the graces of the less developed characteristics. Spiritual growth involves struggling with the temptations of one's root identity and accepting its graces, and coming face-to-face with the many faces of God encountered in the nine personality types.

Dietrich Koller's Enneagram representation of "The Nine Faces of the Soul of Christ" reveals nine different images of God through the life of Jesus.[5] With the soul of Christ, true God and true human at the center of the Enneagram circle, the life of Jesus reveals God as the Perfect One (Type One), as Love (Two), as Creative (Three), as Beautiful (Four), as All-Knowing (Five), as Faithful (Six), as Alive (Seven), as Almighty (Eight), and as Reconciler, Prince of Peace (Nine).

Barbara Metz and John Burchill, in *The Enneagram and Prayer: Discovering Our True Selves before God,* offer multiple scriptural passages for persons in praying through their compulsions, and in entering their path of transformation.[6] For example, Eights are guided to reflect on Second Corinthians 5:14 and to pray that the love of Christ control them and not their image of strictly human power. Praying with Isaiah 61 helps Eights tap into their giftedness of power and advocacy. Eights find strength in John 21:9–19 in letting another be for them. Twos are invited to pray Psalm 103 to assist them in facing God's loving acceptance of their frailty and Mark 9:41 to foster their gift of a free and generous spirit of sharing.

Although the Myers-Briggs and Enneagram personality profiles can be universally applicable, social and cultural conditioning often structure the channel for one's spirituality. The Spirit of God speaks and makes demands through the realities of gender, ethnicity, and sexual circumstances of people's lives. An awareness of the spiritual issues generally impacting white males and females, black men and women, and gays and lesbians enables the companion to be attentive to the social and cultural realities that may shape a seeker's spiritual movement.[7]

In being attentive to these realities, the companion more effectively enters into the world of the seeker, yet does not presume or stereotype the spirituality of any group of people or any member so represented. In being effective, the companion uses her gifts of interpathy and breaks through emotional and/or prejudicial barriers from her own social and cultural conditioning. She becomes freer to ask the seeker what he is going through, to listen to his response, and to offer companionship on his spiritual journey. The companion makes room for the Spirit of God to become more manifest within the seeker's unique reality.

Spirituality of White Men

European American men (by nature and by nurture) form an identity of separateness and autonomy, tend to be aggressive and competitive, and desire to "fix" or make things right. "The male soul thrives on challenge, the heroic, the wild, the individuated."[8]

Conditioned toward the outside world, white men grow spiritually in making peace with their own vulnerability and in developing their intimate and relational characteristics. Men's vulnerability, inherent in their need to be autonomous and to take risks, may be hidden from their self-identity as conditioned by society. Opening themselves to their own vulnerability, men enter the transformative journey of knowing and loving themselves as wounded and able to help others. They become wounded healers.

Through their strength as risk takers, European American men walk the spiritual path of moving from being emotionally distant to developing their more "feminine" or emotionally healthy relational selves. This development is risky in a Western society that often does not value male affection and tenderness except with women who are being "pursued" or within male-female romantic encounters. The spiritual issue for males is to come to an inner conversion of their self-identity as persons who are relational and then to live out of this new identity. Still capable of making hard decisions and able to engage competitively when appropriate, Christian men grow in their capacity for warmth, gentleness, and compassionate caring.

Christian love is sometimes aggressive in moving human reality toward the reign of God. It is not always gentle; it is sometimes fierce and challenging. Many spiritual writers have spoken of the Spirit's burning within them. Scriptural accounts of Pentecost speak of the Spirit as tongues of fire (Acts 2:3). White men's recovery of the fierceness and challenge of Christian love with their spirituality fosters the balance of their gift of aggression and their growth in gentleness and compassion.

Men conditioned toward self-power acted out through personal aggression deal with coming to terms with the power of God within them and with their own power being used for the sake of God and God's work. Within men's spiritual direction God may be inviting them to a new sense of who they are and who God is around the issue of power and authority. Inviting God into their power or writing a dialogue between their power and God's power can be a helpful way of praying for some men in utilizing their aggression and power for the sake of the reign of God.

As white men embrace their vulnerability, they may begin to feel a great sense of pain and loneliness in being perceived as separate, hard workers, and in charge. They may feel this most poignantly within the structure of the Christian church, the place where the life of faith in community is to be nurtured. A hierarchical church structure reinforces male separateness and the notion of men being in charge, yet the church identifies itself as a place of care and nurturance as Holy Mother Church. Men (nonclerics and clerics), sensing the dichotomy between being separate-and-in-charge and being one-with, experience pain in the lack of a place to grow spiritually as men.[9] Christian Scriptures, as well, give little credence to Joseph's role in the life of Jesus. Joseph is perceived as the hard worker outside the relational environment of the home.

Spiritual healing for white men may involve their entering into their pain and loneliness through grieving the loss of connection. This grieving can be facilitated by praying the laments of the Psalms or the book of Lamentations. Moving through their pain (and any associated anger) enables men to make room for the strong self to be renewed and to engage in acts of justice within the church. In brief, the spiritual quest to be a "man of God" for white Christian men is in connecting with themselves, fostering their relational qualities, and being reinvigorated by the strivings of the male soul.

Spirituality of White Women

European American women develop through relationships, taking on concepts from the outside, coming to speak their own voices, and listening to the voices of others. Women are (by nature and nurture) gatherers and community builders; they desire inclusion and equality. For the most part, however, they have been conditioned to be passive and submissive, silent and uninvolved. They have experienced predominantly male language within their Christian churches and God images; women's experiences historically have been ignored, and their social and religious worth has been in their tasks. Thus, white women's spirituality focuses on themselves as valuable in the world of relationships.

A woman's spiritual growth is in claiming her experiences and making the shift from learned dependency and conformity to her true relational self. The spiritual path for women begins by their focusing on their experiences as authoritative, listening to and affirming (and being affirmed in) their humanity through sharing their personal stories. This focusing includes the recognition of the social and personal impacts upon their lives and the restructuring of beliefs about themselves. From viewing power outside the self to reclaiming power in relationships, white women move toward a self-identity as co-creators in furthering the reign of God. The spiritual movement is from allowing external authority to be more powerful than personal inner authority to balancing women's own experience as authoritatively important as that of others. It is a movement toward celebration of the self as God's image while fostering the relational and inclusive. Pride is not the "sin" of white women; women's "sin" is their self-degradation and lack of owning their experience as revelatory of the Divine.

Having adapted to Western male society, white women's identity and spirit have been wounded through being disconnected from the embodied self. Reconnecting with and celebrating the physical being—menstruation, pregnancy, birth, washing, nursing, teaching, cooking, dancing, touching, healing—are part of spiritual healing for women. Women whose bodied selves have been objectified as sex objects, as property for others, as beautified only by thinness and the latest cosmetics, must reclaim their true physicality as expressive of who they are as loved and beloved of God. Their natural spiritual lives are embodied in their whole selves with and for others and self.

As women become more aware of the value of their voices, they may temporarily feel anger at themselves for not appreciating themselves earlier in life. "How could I have thought this way? How could I have let myself be duped?" In growing spiritually, women move out of the self-blame, direct the anger toward the appropriate source, and grow through and beyond the anger to healing. Through their appropriate anger and healing, women become assertively strong, using their gifts as gatherers and community builders to confront injustices and to call others into dialogue to find the truth.

In their spiritual journey women begin to reimage God and to discover many wonderful scriptural images of God that relate to their experiences. They often benefit in a powerful way from having dialogues with women absent from the scriptural accounts as well as women in scripture whom the church has not included liturgically. Finding and celebrating themselves as women with women and with men heal and enhance women's spirits.

Spirituality of African Americans

African American spirituality is African and American.[10] It is based on an African worldview and on the experiences of a people in America. Africans value the interrelatedness and interdependency of all within the world. African identity is within a group where responsibility is collective among all as brothers and sisters. The Africans have a proverb that says, "I am because we are, and because we are, therefore, I am." Within this worldview the concept of spirit is central and includes the influences of the unborn, the living, and the dead. The spirit of those to come and those who have passed on is as active as those now living. The African spirit is intensely aware of the presence of God being everywhere and of the connection of everything—intellect, emotions, and sentiments.

As a people who experienced slavery in America, African American men and women have a rich tradition of hope and trust in God's promises to liberate God's people. In the midst of oppression, African American spirituality is one of a "people on the way," a people of hope in the midst of hopelessness. Their Christian spirituality is grounded in the Hebrew and Christian Scriptures as a record of the stories of God delivering God's people from bondage and oppression. The Bible often serves as a form of survival and deliverance for a people who in slavery learned that God is not a respecter of persons. African American "spirituals" born out of slavery consistently affirm the presence of God in reality no matter what and identify the inner peace of black spirituality that is frequently expressed in the interconnection of body, mind, and soul through emotional release. The truth will set them free (John 8:32).

The wholeness of Jesus—his humanity—is of central significance for blacks; Jesus as liberator and confronter of oppressive systems is the focal point of black Christians. The call to discipleship for the African American spirit is "to remember their past, to engage in the present, and to prepare for the future—a future free from oppressions and free to live out God's promises in this world."[11]

African American spiritual growth may include pride in blackness, proclamation of a Spirit of freedom, and the reclamation of collective responsibility within the family and among one another. In *Black Looks: Race and Representation,* bell hooks connects the spirit of blacks to one of resistance to the internalization of images given them by white America, a spirit alive in the Spirit resisting political oppression.[12] In the strength of their black spirit as a people of resistance, African Americans move beyond a sense of having to defend attacks to a groundedness in a life of justice of right relationships among themselves and among others. What were viewed as personal attacks are now viewed as total social disharmony (all peoples are affected by social issues) and a disconnectedness from God's intentions for all humanity. The spiritual movement of African Americans encompasses not only an embrace of their African and collective identity as a people but also a recognition of their place in the building of social justice for the sake of the reign of God. Spiritual growth empowers the African American within a people and as an individual.

African American women's spirituality is based on a positive view of the concept of matriarch, a reality that has given black women a spirit of strength, perseverance, and determination.[13] Liberation for the "womanist" person is an identity within a group, a coming together of many "I's," and is distinct from liberation for white women (recognized in the feminist movement), which is centered in an identity of individuated self.

"A womanist then is a strong Black woman who has sometimes been mis-labeled as a domineering, castrating matriarch. A womanist is one who has developed survival strategies in spite of the oppression of her race and sex in order to save her family and her people."[14] Unlike white women who learn to surpass the liberation of their mothers from patriarchy, black women strive to continue the tradition of strength found in their elders. Vulnerability for African American women is generally not an option as it is in the white community. Through exploitation by white men, white women, and black men, black women often have no certainty that they will be taken care of by anyone other than themselves.

Black women's spirituality comes out of a tradition of marginalization and stereotyping. The black woman has been controlled by being imaged as the dutiful, submissive "mammy" for white employers, the powerful, dominating matriarch who sacrifices physically for her children while neglecting their emotional and social needs by her absence, the welfare mom who sits around doing nothing, and the nonsexual whore or sexually aggressive one. Black women have coped in society by expecting the worst, surrendering to God, sparing others, and finding strength in a community of faith.

Black women's spiritual way is to claim and affirm their strength, power, and resilience as matriarch, and to search for the meaning of their faith in Jesus in light of their unique experiences of discrimination, poverty, isolation, and infant deaths. In claiming appropriately their positive identity as matriarchs, womanists can move from a sense of living solely by survival strategies to a place of strength and closeness in mutuality with others. The spiritual need of the womanist, as Teresa Snorton maintains, is not in being changed but in seeking intimacy.[15]

Spirituality of Gays and Lesbians

Spirituality of gays and lesbians is a coming home within oneself and within community, in being transformed from being outsiders to finding the sacred place of wholeness for which they yearn. It is a spirituality flowing from their experiences of loss and the shattering of traditional Christian images. "The self is complete when the lesbian or gay being images her or his core as holy and merged with the Divine."[16]

Many gay men and lesbians of all cultural and ethnic groups have experienced a loss of belonging, a loss of being identified with a people with whom they feel at home. This deep loss has resulted from their being discriminated against and often ostracized from family, society, and faith community because of their sexual preferences. Many also have often lost lovers and friends who died with HIV/AIDS. Having found a new community and support system (and often church), gays and lesbians continually confront loss and separation.

Being treated as outsiders in a world and religious system that is all too often closed to listening to, dialoguing with, and valuing their experiences, many gays and lesbians feel a deep sense of brokenness and shame. Their spiritual journey of coming home within themselves and within community can be an invitation to explore the Christian Scriptures and Christian beliefs around good and evil, grace and sin. Too many have heard from their Christian communities and families that they are evil and sin personified.

Issues of good and evil, grace and sin may be associated with a fundamental understanding of the human person as embodied and as sexual. Gays and lesbians, having heard little or no positive Christian interpretations of sexuality, may struggle against internalizing negative images of themselves. Being in dialogue with nonjudgmental companions aware of their own sexual being and for whom Christian sexual ethics is important, lesbians and gays can experience grace and goodness. They are able to affirm and be affirmed in their sense of the goodness of the body and of sexuality, and to make appropriate choices in sexual behavior.

Persons feeling shame, conditioned to feel that they are mistakes because of their sexuality, can find healing by attending to questions around their identity. "If I am created in the image of God and unconditionally loved by God, then who is this God if I am gay or lesbian?" "Do I represent God?" "What images of God no longer fit?" "What is my experience of God and of myself when I allow myself to be seen by God?"

Persons broken through loss find healing in entering the grieving process, in experiencing and expressing to a caring, compassionate person their emotional pain and the impact of all that was lost. Through their grieving appropriately, gays and lesbians can find new energy for living and for coming to the truth about who they are as persons whom God loves and does not abandon. They make room within themselves to experience grace and freedom in relating with and living committed to Christian truths as persons who are gay and lesbian.

Along their spiritual walk, some Christian gay men and lesbians relate with the suffering Jesus. Through their experiences of discrimination and rejection, gays and lesbians experience a God of promise in the life, death, and resurrection of Jesus who walks with them in pain and struggle; they can proclaim their yes to God in and through Jesus Christ. Through an identity with the God of promise, lesbians and gays deepen their love of God and find God's love in them. Through this greater depth of love, gay men and lesbians are freed to break from the bounds of the false images given to them and to come to appreciate their true selves. Their lives of love in and with God enable them to be disciples of Christ in confronting religious and civil authorities as cocreators with the Divine.

In this phase of their spiritual journey, lesbians and gay men enter into a period of self-emptying that profoundly affects the work of Christianity in addressing social, political, and religious evils. The transforming grace of love accepted by gay men and lesbians moves them through self-concern and anger to a passion for social justice for the sake of God's reign; grace moves them toward a generativity of compassion and care that goes beyond themselves. A spirituality of gays and lesbians involves coming into their own identity and creating new images for themselves and others within the truths and biblical concepts of the Christian community.[17]

Conclusion

Companioning a Christian seeker on his spiritual journey is a holy and sacred event. Being with another in faith as God reveals God's self to him includes being aware of the paths of personality and spiritual development. In her awareness, the companion listens within the context of the seeker, while ultimately attending to the seeker and the word of God being revealed through how he interprets and experiences his unique reality.

Questions for Reflection

1. What has been your spiritual direction?
2. How would you define spiritual development?
3. What new awareness have you gained through reading this chapter?
4. What prejudices do you bring to spiritual companioning?
5. What characteristic of God do you need at this time of your life?
6. What areas from this chapter would be good for you to gain more knowledge, experience, and/or reflection about? How will you gain what you need?

Spend some time journaling your thoughts and feelings. At the end of journaling, choose your favorite scriptural passage or your favorite prayer from another source and pray that passage or prayer. Return to the prayer you wrote at the end of chapter 1. Do you want to pray it now, or is it time to write a new prayer?

Part 3: Issues in Spiritual Companionship

chapter 8

Guilt and Shame

G uilt and shame are significant emotions directly related to individuals' coresponsibility as created to live in society and to grow in the image of God. Guilt is essential to moral existence. Shame is a fundamental emotion connected to a true identity of the self. As such, healthy guilt and shame are critical issues in the spiritual life of persons.

Developing a more authentic or true self in relating with the self and with God includes the awareness and healing of unhealthy guilt and shame and the affirmation and activation of healthy guilt and shame. In her being with the seeker, the spiritual companion is attentive to issues around guilt and shame that create a resistance for him in his becoming more fully human. The companion provides the seeker with a caring, nonjudgmental presence and offers him ways of praying with and owning both guilt and shame. Through the companion relationship, the seeker can find healing strength within these emotions, allow release of any barriers to his freedom and growth, and experience authentic grace in becoming more fully human.

Guilt and Shame

Healthy guilt and shame are part of the developmental cycle and are learned initially in early childhood. Guilt is associated with the establishment of values and beliefs; shame is developed through the awareness of who one is. Through appropriate parenting, individuals learn what actions or behaviors are right or wrong and who they are as human beings.

Most psychological theorists maintain that the development of shame precedes the development of guilt. Appropriate guilt is formed out of the need to be loved and to be in right relationships with others. Appropriate shame is fostered through dynamics of affection, acceptance, and positive valuation by those in charge of one's growth. Healthy guilt emerges from a healthy sense of shame and leads to acting responsibly, expressing regrets and repentance, and receiving forgiveness. Healthy shame is an emotion reminding humans of their disharmony with self, others, and God, which affects discretion in making choices in life.

- Guilt affects one's interpersonal life; shame affects one's intrapersonal and interpersonal life.
- Guilt is an emotion about one's actions; shame refers to the feeling one has about the self.
- Feelings of guilt emerge from an unconscious threat of punishment when one's behavior violates boundaries established as normative; shame is generated from a fear of separation or abandonment when one feels an inadequacy or failure in the achievement of a desired internal self-concept.

David Augsburger identifies shame as containing a bipolar system: it separates and presses for reunion; it is an impulse to conceal and a yearning to be accepted; it fosters responsibility toward others and creates personal recognition of a need to respond in more acceptable ways.[1]

The Adam and Eve story depicting the tension to cope with being with the Divine and being separate from the Divine illustrates humanity's defensive mechanisms against appearing naked before God.[2] The story disavows the experience of shame in life by covering it up (with a fig leaf). Healthy shame and guilt perceive the self as frail and vulnerable before God and deeply loved despite human finiteness. In this context, James Bowler in the article "Shame: A Primary Root of Resistance to Movement in Direction" proposes that Christian theology may be better served by speaking of "original shame" instead of "original sin," viewing Jesus as "coming to save humankind from original shame."[3]

Many circumstances have led individuals to defenses against who they are before God by their being "shamed" into false identities; they have acquired "toxic" shame, feeling disgraced and guilt ridden. These circumstances present barriers to one's spiritual growth as truly human created in the image of God. Debilitating guilt results from disgrace or disabling shame. These same circumstances are the ground for the personality individuals adapt and from which spiritual growth is born. The Enneagram typology is a good tool in growing spiritually with one's survival patterns and messages from early life.

Origins of Disgraced Shame and Guilt

In its explanation of human self-consciousness, family systems theory points to the origins of unhealthy shame (disgrace) as rooted in the family. The child learns about who one is through the mirroring of parents or the persons under whom the child developed an identity. Children whose primary needs were not met received a message that they are not important; they do not matter. Children who hear—directly, indirectly, privately, publicly— "don't feel," "don't think," "don't talk," "don't assert yourself," "don't make mistakes," learn to suppress who they really are and adapt an identity of "I am a mistake" or "I am nothing."

These children feel normal developmental anxiety or fear in being cared for, yet this anxiety is exacerbated in light of the external restraints to their personhood. Fear of punishment overrides normal anxiety, and a cycle of suppression of self and repression of feelings develops around a shame-based identity and actions motivated by guilt. Instead of anger being expressed at the controls from outside, anger is repressed, anxiety for survival is heightened, guilt for feeling the anger and wanting to be themselves is introjected, and individuals feel shame at their anger and guilt. To feel anger means to face potential abandonment of the adults needed by the child. The helpless feeling that is experienced when one is shamed gets trapped in this cycle and is maintained well into adulthood if not healed. The inner child of the adult remains wounded. Both the insight into who one is truly and the awareness of a range of appropriate behaviors are thwarted. Guilt that says, "What I did was not right; I regret that and ask forgiveness," becomes distorted into, "I can be good only if I am perfect, follow all the rules legalistically, and do my duty." Persons growing up in shame-based or guilt-based environments internalize shame and guilt, which they carry into adulthood.

Other family dynamics affecting how persons perceive themselves in relation to themselves, others, and God are associated with the roles individuals played in the family of origin and the position they had in the family. Children sometimes take on roles within the family that are inconsistent with the role of a child; they take on the adult roles that parents are not able to manage or that are forbidden. Such roles are placater or peacemaker, boss, rescuer, calm observer, distractor, or comedian when tension occurs.

By taking on such roles, children learn a self that is not themselves. The spontaneous, free, and participating self is suppressed, and feelings are hidden deep within them. Children triangulated between mom and dad by having to communicate the messages of one parent to the other learn that they are not unique individuals and adapt roles associated with speaking for others. Mom and dad are unable to model healthy communication and decision making as adults and use the child as go-between.

Adults, who as children experienced physical and/or sexual abuse, suffered emotionally as well. Those physically abused want out of the situation yet have nowhere to go. They cease identifying with themselves and begin, out of the fear of abandonment, to identify with the parent taking on a "bad child" identification as one who is defective and flawed. To survive sexual abuse, many children take on a separate identity that helps them be emotionally detached from the event that is out of their control. The survivor's identity is a powerful and useful self in adulthood, yet the true self is hidden, particularly if the abuse took place over an extended period of time.

Children reared by a narcissistic parent (mother in particular for girls) learn to meet the narcissistic needs of the parent while not getting their own ego needs met. While having to parent their parent, these children grow into an identity that rejects a healthy sense of self as needy, and they feel ashamed or guilty in having needs. Healthy shame contains emotional energy that moves persons to get their needs met based on reliable structures and boundaries that ensure those interpersonal structures.

In physical, sexual, and emotional abuse, boundaries between parent (or other adult) and child are violated. While healthy shame pushes individuals to a self-identity that is limited in relation to self, others, and God, abusive shame results when boundaries are so diffused that one does not know limits or when they are so rigid that the person becomes entrapped emotionally. Individuals so shamed neither view the self as a core boundary ("I am okay and have control over my physical, emotional, sexual self") nor perceive anything about themselves as okay. Guilt in transgressing their values turns into the thought, *I have no right to my values and desires except through my rigid role or performance skills.*

Persons reared in a culture in which maternal dependency and bonding are paramount to parenting are shamed when punishment is given through ostracism from the mother. Children locked out of the house or refused maternal attention for a period of time are given negative and mixed messages about the boundaries with the mother. These many complex boundary dilemmas occur in different degrees and are not the only sources of individuals' unhealthy shame and guilt.

Social conditioning outside the family greatly affects one's internalization of shame and guilt.

- The experiences of persons of color have given them messages within Western society that they are not valued and worthwhile. Receiving negative messages from almost every realm of their social lives, persons internalize them as an unconscious means of survival; they begin to identify with worthlessness.
- Gay men and lesbians, told they do not belong because of their sexual preferences, may be forced to internalize a negative self-concept in order to function within the social structures.
- Young boys and girls becoming aware of their sexual selves are prone particularly to this internalization from a lack of support in discussing their sexual tendencies with trusted adults.
- Persons treated socially, racially, or ethnically as inferior feel the shame of discrimination.
- Persons with disabilities—physical or mental—can feel shame in anticipation of going to public places or a shame of imperfection given to them by society.

When shame is internalized from parental or societal factors (including religious systems), it no longer functions in its positive power of discretion;

it becomes a characteristic style of the person. The authentic and private self gets smaller, and the self connected with the shame identification becomes larger. In its negative form as an offshoot of disgrace, guilt has the power to destroy a person's inner peace. The positive power of confession, repentance, and forgiveness is lost to the negative power of guilt. Instead of the power of reaffirming one's values and beliefs through which growth is promoted, negative guilt hampers one's growth.

Although there is no such reality as a "shame culture" or a "guilt culture," certain cultural influences impact individuals' personality type and support a dominance of shame or guilt in the lives of the members. Persons in a culture believing that individuals are in charge of their lives and have power to determine their life courses regardless of external social systems will be more prone to guilt than shame. Persons who view themselves as defined by others and believe that they have little personal control of their lives are equally more prone to guilt than shame; powerlessness and self-blame (guilt) are prevalent. Persons, for example, living on the margins of Western society because of cultural racism can internalize the messages of society, rejecting their own value and internalizing the guilt placed upon them. They may come to believe societal messages that they are "lazy," "inferior," and "worthless" and feel guilty for being that way; they blame themselves for not being able to change personally their reality.

Individuals influenced by a worldview that values one's personal ability to shape and manage life's events and perceives external social systems responsible for any barriers to one's goals are more prone to feel shame than guilt. Such persons within Western society are minority groups who take pride in their racial, gender, sexual, and cultural heritage over against the majority's definition of them. Shame is felt when these individuals experience themselves as unable to shape their lives in the midst of external forces; they feel inadequate in their being. Persons who perceive themselves as having no options within social strata—they are defined by others who have full responsibility for life—are prone to live lives characterized by shame. Those discriminated against sexually, economically, religiously, and socially bear the burden of disabling shame that disempowers their true self-identity. People among the latter group are also prone to depression; they perceive themselves as objects of others, with no self-identity and no responsibility.

Western culture places high value on performance, particularly for men and women in positions of authority. Not performing according to the external standards may trigger early life shame that is part of the inner dynamic of the adult. "Shoulds" are commonly internalized within the Western society. Internal shame within the Western culture is understood as how persons feel when they do not live up to their expectations of themselves.

Asian cultures speak of "saving face." In these cultures, more emphasis is placed on the individual's role for the sake of the whole. "Saving face" is maintaining proper role functioning to avoid public ridicule or loss of union with the group. In "losing face" one feels a sense of public shame or social embarrassment in not living up to the community's rules and expectations. Public shame involves the fear of losing face before others; private shame is the internalization of the group norms and values. Internal shame occurs when one has caused harm to a community member or to others upon whom one has relied. "Saving face" is deep within these cultures and accompanies a sense of self-identity; internal shame functions in the building of harmony and group unity.[4]

Masks That Defend Shame and Guilt

There is, within the human, a sense that if one were really known, one would not be loved and cared for. If the truth of oneself were known, one would not survive this truth; the evil that was learned or done is thought to be greater than the good of the person. Disgrace is taught, and the only self one knows through unhealthy shame and guilt is a false self; the true self has been suppressed. Many persons have adopted masks (fig leaves) to conceal their shame or guilt in their encounters with others, self, and God. Persons hide—consciously and unconsciously—from God out of fear of not measuring up (not being okay) or out of fear of being punished (not doing okay).

One way to cloak shame is to project self-sufficiency and no need for others. A sense of self-righteousness demonstrated in perfectionism, judgment, and blame is another way to hide behind unhealthy shame. One sees the speck in another's eye yet misses the log in one's own eye. Many times this self-righteousness is spiritualized and done in the name of Christianity. For example, a person may view herself as knowing the mind of God and behave as if she alone has the truth for everyone. "God has clearly said . . ." In reality, this person may be acting out of her desires to control others and using God to back her up.

Shame's close connection to one's inner identity makes it harder to deal with directly than with guilt, a more overt emotion. Shame tends to be converted into the more overt feelings of resentment, grief, and anger. The resentment, grief, and anger need to be recognized and viewed as possible cover-ups for unhealed shame or guilt from shame. Others cover their shame in depression. Not being able to break the cycle learned earlier in life when anger at being shamed was suppressed, a person turns the unexpressed guilt into depression. Shame cannot live with the unlovable, unprotected, and undefended. Persons with this form of depression may need psychiatric assistance as well as spiritual companioning if the depression is persistent and has become a mode of life.

Shame can be masked through alcoholism, drug addictions, and other forms of self-destructive behaviors. The message underlying these addictive behaviors, sometimes learned from the family as normative, is, "I am not okay, so why care for myself? Nobody cares, so why should I? I am nothing." Though the Alcoholics Anonymous (AA) format has been criticized as disempowering for persons to develop a free identity in its perpetuation of "recovering," it points to the basics of shame. The first step of AA is to admit that one is powerless and needs the help of the Higher Power.

One of the most prevalent forms of guilt and shame masking is the numbing of feelings. The unconscious (and, sometimes, conscious) decision persons make to survive feelings of guilt and shame is to shut down emotionally. Many persons, shame-based from childhood, have learned that feelings do not matter. Persons' roles within a family may warrant this adaptive behavior. For example, a person's role as placater perpetuates one's identity as conflict avoider and enhances guilt when in the midst of conflict; the individual loses the positive power of living through conflict by being overwhelmed with feelings of guilt or shame.

Adults who have developed a sense of shame and guilt often create a triangular drama when confronted with difficult or tense circumstances. They perceive the interpersonal relationship within these events as the interplay between a victim, a perpetrator, and a blamer. They perceive themselves in one of the three roles and experience others (including systems) in the other two roles. Personal role identity is switched unconsciously in different circumstances, provoking their internalized shame or guilt.

For example, an individual may feel victimized by a person in authority (the perpetrator) because of one's workplace structure (the system is blamed). At another time, under the duress of shame or guilt, this same person may victimize the boss by rude and curt remarks when one's ideas are not incorporated in the company's programs (individual becomes perpetrator, boss is victimized, company is blamed for the lack of acceptance). This relational drama masks shame and/or guilt that is rooted in one's personality and from which one has not found a safe milieu.

Spiritualizing shame and guilt also serves as a defensive mask. Operating out of an image of God as taskmaster or judge, individuals mask by maintaining a strong resistance to images of God that speak of God's affection and value for the individual. Individuals may strongly hold to the power of being unworthy ("O God, I am not worthy") in the face of God. One may focus on being "a mere worm." God, they maintain, is so far superior to them that they must remain inferior. The personal God of Christianity is beyond any relational possibility for them.

Healing through Spiritual Companioning

A critical task of the Christian spiritual journey is the healing of the false self and the undertaking of substantial changes to one's way of being a self. The process of this Christian journey begins with facing the false and true selves through which the seeker recaptures for the true self the energies spent in defending shame and guilt. The recognition and recapturing occur in the acknowledgment and exposure of one's felt defect or lack to a trusted other.

This healing of disgrace involves the recognition and acceptance of the true self as flawed, vulnerable, and limited as human created in the image of God and the dismantling of the false self one has shaped in managing life. It is a conversion to genuine human identity (a humility grounded in truth), to healthy shame that is discretionary and healthy guilt based on Christian values of community. Fully accepting oneself and recognizing the shadow or undeveloped side of one's personality (through Myers-Briggs or Enneagram work) are major starting points in this spiritual conversion process.

For the Christian seeker, the starting point may be the discovery that he is no longer cooperating with God as well as he once had been. The seeker feels a sense of disharmony with God that is God's invitation for him to move toward a truer self-identity in the encounter of healthy shame. In accepting God's invitation, the seeker grows by confronting his avoidance (shadow) in relating with God, self, and others. In his self-confrontation, the seeker's defenses break down, and he is able to redefine new values and priorities in concert with a truer self-identity. Through this process of conversion, one comes home to the true self, to grace, and to God.

The spiritual companion walks with the seeker in owning his resistance and behaviors that mask his true self. She accompanies him in his praying with the false self and gently offers assistance in his conversion. Her nonjudgmental presence and unconditional love mirror for the seeker his acceptance and provide a safe place for him to name underlying shame issues. Being attentive to the seeker's self-expression, the companion may ask, "Could you tell me more about who you are (what role you play) in this circumstance?" or "It sounds as if you might fear God's abandoning you or punishing you; is that correct?" as a way of opening up issues around shame or guilt.

The companion's reception of the seeker's response and her gentle invitation to explore the reality of his identity lay the groundwork for his conversion. Guided by the tools of the Myers-Briggs or Enneagram, the companion can provide a consistent focus for her being with the other. In her guidance, the companion reflects privately on how she is maintaining appropriate emotional boundaries in following the pace the seeker is choosing to walk. She does not push the seeker beyond his limit setting; she invites gently and consistently, yet not aggressively.

The Hebrew Scriptures contain approximately 150 references to shame and few to guilt. Psalm 31 as a prayer and praise for deliverance from the enemy of shame is a good reference to pray with. Psalm 32 is a prayer of the joy of forgiveness that can help the seeker. The Christian Scriptures deal with the healing of shame and guilt in their focus on God's incarnation, forgiveness, acceptance, and liberation through Jesus. They make a bold claim on true intimacy with God and the inclusion of all in the community of grace. The Gospels show Jesus committed to the healing of shame.

The paschal mystery of Christian faith grounds the work of healing and the birthing of one as truly human created in God's image and likeness. "For one believes with the heart and so is justified, and one confesses with the mouth and so is saved. . . . 'No one who believes . . . will be put to shame.' For there is no distinction. . . . The same God is God of all and is generous to all who call on God" (Rom. 10:10–12).

Questions for Reflection

1. What messages did you receive about yourself in early childhood?

2. What masks do you wear to hide shame and guilt?

3. In your spiritual journey, how have you confronted your masks and faced your false self and true self?

4. Where are there unhealthy shame and guilt in your life today?

5. Are you a person who can be with others in their shame and guilt without judging, blaming, or criticizing negatively?

6. Are you able to be vulnerable before God and others?

Pray separately Psalms 31 and 32, and contemplate the paschal mystery. What is God's invitation to you today?

chapter 9

Sin and Forgiveness

The Judeo-Christian tradition affirms humanity's ability to do good and to do evil, to be loving and to be unloving, to know mercy and to give mercy, to be guilty of sin yet loved beyond guilt and sin. Human beings live within a communal reality affected with sin and God's grace of being forgiven. Humanity is always within the loving embrace of God and being moved by the Spirit toward wholeness and life in communal loving relationship. Divine grace exceeds the power of sin. Created good by a good and loving God, human beings are drawn through God's gift of grace to fullness in the image of the Creator. Christian faith trusts that God desires human goodness, is within human experience, and can act decisively in a broken world.

A fundamental spiritual task of the Christian seeker, therefore, is to reflect upon how his life with all its possibilities builds a life of love and where, at what point, through what causes, does his life rupture the creation of God's reign. This spiritual task is that of discerning whether one's life is lived in response to the Spirit or in response to someone or something other than the indwelling Spirit; it is the discerning of how one is living from the true self. This task involves one's openness to divine and human forgiveness in the recognition of one's sinfulness and of one's ability to grow lovingly through interpersonal reconciliation.

The spiritual seeker comes to a greater knowledge of God's relationship with him and of himself in becoming aware of his sinfulness and ability to be forgiven by God and others and to forgive. The seeker's recognition of his participation in sin and forgiveness serves as a moment of spiritual transformation for him. In the concrete realization of sinfulness and forgiveness, the seeker is better able to develop a sense of himself as human and to live in loving relationship with others grounded in God's loving care of him. The seeker becomes better able to live a life of reconciliation and right relationships in imitation of Jesus.

The task of the spiritual companion is to help the seeker grow through his reality as one who sins and is forgiven. Her task is to take seriously the seeker, deal realistically with his reality by bearing his burdens with him, and be a sustaining, loving presence that fosters the seeker's movement toward reconciliation and restoration with God and others. This task challenges the companion to reflect on how sinfulness and forgiveness are operative in her life. It also challenges her to examine the depth of her true identity as human in relationship with God and her Christian commitment in relationship with others. An awareness of the nature of sin and of forgiveness will assist the companion in fulfilling her task of being with the spiritual seeker.

Sin

The nature of sin rests within the context of the nature of human beings created and sustained in God's self-communicating love. Sin is understood theologically in the light of divine love that nourishes and draws persons to become their authentic or true selves created in God's image and likeness.

God chose to create human beings out of God's desire to pour out divine love in creation, in incarnation, in the ordinariness of human life. God chose to communicate God's self in Jesus for the purpose of sharing divine love. Through this divine outpouring of love, God's everlasting presence makes possible and sustains an operative power of love within each person; human beings' ability to love and to care is made possible by their first being loved by God. God's initiation of love creates within human beings a freedom to love God, the self, and others. Created in God's love, persons, in their deepest nature and authentic selves, live in a freedom that orients them toward God in being loving.

Though fundamentally oriented to choose love, persons misuse their freedom in choosing what is contrary to an authentic life of love; they choose to live disconnected from their basic orientation of love in God. This misuse of freedom deadens the spirit of love that constitutes authentic human beingness. Sin exists when persons think they are all that there is and are, therefore, divine; humans deny the Other and believe their own order is the reign of God. Sin is not actions per se but the attitude about human reality underlying human behavior and relationships with all of creation. This attitude is always expressed in actions. Sin is, ultimately, saying no to God; persons choose to live outside divine love. The manifestation of sin is demonstrated through personal, universal, and systemic/structural realities in the world of human existence. Evil of sin is within humanity, the spiritual powers of the universe, and social institutions; evil is within human beings (designated in the Jungian "shadow") and among them (as "collective shadow").

The Genesis story of the Fall is an account of the threefold aspect of evil through humanity's misuse of its freedom in choosing to live separate from divine love. Genesis 3 is the story of human beings', man's and woman's, willful rebellion against God; human sin first entered the world through personal human choice to live outside the presence of the Creator. Personal sin of man and woman creates a rupture in the life of the Spirit within the very life of the universe. "God saw that the wickedness of humankind was great in the earth, and that every inclination of the thoughts of their hearts was only evil continually" (Gen. 6:5). Genesis 11 tells the story of the sin of the nations of people in their building their own city out of protection and self-interest: "Come, let us build ourselves a city, and a tower with its top in the heavens, and let us make a name for ourselves; otherwise we shall be scattered abroad upon the face of the whole earth" (Gen. 11:4).[1]

Born into a world influenced by the power of God's self-communicating love, each person, because of the collective nature of sin, is also born into a world marked by the power of sin. Before an individual becomes able to make choices in directing one's life toward God, each person is affected by the power of God's love *and* the power of sin inherent in the accumulated sins of the community throughout history. One originally enters the world bound spiritually by the result of the sins of others; sin (original sin) is inherited through the prevalence of the power of sin in the world into which one is born. Thus, human life is situated in the tension between a world of grace in the power of Jesus and a world of sin. Within this tension, human authenticity is revealed in persons' choices to live in the power of God's grace and in rejection of the ways of sin that separate them from their creation in and with God. The authentic self is an openness and response to the dynamism of the Divine in all of one's life.

Personal sin is a manifestation of an individual being closed to the power of God within one and all creation. It is a personal orientation, attitude, or act that involves a rejection of God's love and a false love of a creature due to the misuse of personal freedom. Social sin is the dimension of a whole people (a system or structure) closed to divine love in choosing self-interests in disregard for the community; caught in the power of sin in the world, people live disassociated from the indwelling Spirit.

Freedom rooted in the power of divine love is used, personally and collectively, in a way that breaks the covenanted relationship of God with God's people. Individuals and groups of people sin in living out of an attitude of the self (or selves) as the force and power in building reality. Human beings, living now in the "garden" of good (grace) and evil, sin by choosing to create their own categories of wrong and right; they choose to become something other than human, to be something they are not. Transgression from the way of God does not rest exclusively in one's actions but is associated with one's primary disposition toward God.

Since sin is associated with one's fundamental attitude, persons seeking to grow spiritually must enter into an examination of their lives according to the standards upon which they act. Accepting the reality of human capability of sin, Christians can easily overlook the real dimension of sin in their lives by avoiding an honest examination of their underlying desires, egotistical concerns, and values precipitating their actions.

For example, one may choose a good act and undermine it by an evil motivation. One may feed the hungry at a soup kitchen (a very good act) in order to be seen as good or in order to be accepted by someone. Or an institution may give everyone a raise not from a sense of justice but from a desire to avoid union activity.

A spiritual seeker may readily identify that he has lied to his friend; he is repentant of a "venial" sin. Yet this recognition of lying may be a clear cover-up for a more basic attitude of rejection of God in his life. In the admission of lying the seeker may be excusing himself from looking at his underlying motivation of superiority or grandiosity in relation to others. Social sin can also be overlooked because of the human tendency to find a particular "devil" who is transgressing God's law of love and justice. Focus on individuals can enable a person to ignore the social or corporate sin of institutional policies and actions. "Everyone seems nice" can be a mask to naming the social sin of unloving relationships manifested through systems and structures; individual relationships hide the collective (corporate) sin of an institution. In hiding from sin persons shelter themselves from their true authentic selves and from their Christian commitment to confront the sin of the world as justice-making people.

Both the Hebrew and the Christian Scriptures teach that sin provokes divine judgment that does not destroy humanity but is meant to awaken humanity to the devastating truth of a life of sin. Divine judgment is an assessment of reality born out of God's covenanted love with humanity and calls individuals to reconciliation through repentance and forgiveness. Exodus reveals that shortly after God established the covenant on Mount Sinai, the people turned away from God's command by setting up false images. God named the people's sin and shared with Moses God's wrath and desire to consume the people, instructing him to go down at once to the people and tell them of their sin. Feeling God's wrath at the reality of the sins of the people, Moses pleaded with God, reminding God of divine goodness. Hearing the repentant plea of Moses grounded on his faith in a good God, God renegotiated the covenant (Exod. 32–34). Reconciliation occurred through God's forgiveness of the stiff-necked people.

The Christian Scriptures are filled with examples of divine judgment upon those who choose to live outside the power of grace. "Woe to you, scribes and Pharisees, hypocrites!...Woe to you, blind guides.... Woe to you ... for you tithe mint, dill, and cummin, and have neglected the weightier matters of the law: justice and mercy and faith. . . . Woe to you. . . . You are like whitewashed tombs" (Matt. 23:13–27). In his teaching that all are sinners, Jesus reminds his followers that "unless you repent, you will all perish" (Luke 13:3).

In the story of the sinful woman anointing Jesus' feet, Jesus confronts the objecting Pharisees with their lack of repentant love that leads to recognition of divine forgiveness and restoration of true relationship with God. "Therefore, I tell you, her sins, which were many, have been forgiven; hence she has shown great love. But the one to whom little is forgiven, loves little" (Luke 7:47).

In proclaiming through the Beatitudes the reign of God as a reversal to the way people were acting, Jesus says,

> *Blessed are you who are poor,*
> *for yours is the reign of God.*
> *Blessed are you who are hungry. . . .*
> *But woe to you who are rich,*
> *for you have received your consolation. . . .*
> *Woe to you who are full now,*
> *for you will be hungry. . . .*
> *Woe to you when all speak well of you, for that is what their ancestors did to*
> *the false prophets. (Luke 6:24–26)*

When the spiritual seeker is able to name and to see sin within himself, he becomes more awakened to God's relationship with him. For, as Paul teaches, the grace of God abounds all the more where sin abounds (Rom. 5:20). To know the wonders of grace, one must experience the reality of sin. Unlike human love that is between two finite beings, God's love does not come and go depending on one's response. The Spirit continually renews the face of the earth (Ps. 104:30). God searches for those who have lost their way as a woman does for a misplaced coin (Luke 15:8–10).

God's everlasting love continually sustains individuals and peoples in their fundamental stance in freedom to love, to move toward God. God looks not on outer cleanliness, but on the heart (see Mark 1:40–45) and offers divine grace that gives humanity the possibility of choosing to change the way things are going.

> *Who is a God like you, pardoning iniquity*
> *and passing over the transgression . . . ?*
> *Who will again have compassion upon us. . . .*
> *You will cast all our sins into the depths of the sea.*
> *You will show faithfulness. (Mic. 7:18–20)*

Forgiveness

Forgiveness is based on love and restores people to a life lived in right relationship with God. Forgiveness transforms persons' lives more in the direction of God. The real focus of forgiveness spoken of in scripture is not on a release from guilt or a proof of human goodness; God's love (agape) reconciles people to wholeness and life in the community of all peoples. In response to their inquiry of how to pray, Jesus teaches his followers to pray for the reign of God to come in the daily bread of their being forgiven of sins as they forgive one another (Luke 11:2–4).

The primary importance is the affirmation of God's relationship with the person praying and not on the acts of the sins.[2] Scriptures also tell us of the necessity for dealing realistically with sin and repentance in being transformed through forgiveness. God saw the sins of the Israelites. Jesus identified the woman anointing his feet as a person with many sins. The transformation of the woman at the well included the reality that Jesus "told me everything I have ever done" (John 4:39). Repentance symbolizes concretely the way God transforms sinners. Persons are transformed through an interior change.

The Christian Scriptures are the story of God's healing of brokenness through Jesus who responded to the faith of the people. "When Jesus saw their faith, he said to the paralytic, 'Take heart, son; your sins are forgiven'" (Matt. 9:2). The faith Jesus speaks of, here and in other accounts, is not so much a blind belief in him but a belief that God can act decisively in the midst of human brokenness and sin. The miracles of healing are the miracles of reconciliation, of bringing people into oneness with God and with the community; they are miracles pointing to sinfulness forgiven. To be open to God's power of forgiveness/reconciliation is to trust that God is present among us and desires to act on our behalf.

Forgiveness is a step along the way to true reconciliation and renewal of right relationships of being loved and loving. True forgiveness is possible, then, when reconciliation is experienced as possible. Reconciliation with God is always possible in our world of the grace of God's love. Freedom understood within God's unconditional love draws each person toward divine reconciliation. One does not need to try to be forgiven; forgiveness is discovered in facing one's reality as human. The good news of Jesus is that the inherent power of God's self-communicating love transcends the inherent power of evil.

Human Forgiveness

Christian life is one of forgiveness and reconciliation. Jesus, who came not to abolish the law or the prophets but to fulfill them, teaches that "in everything do to others as you would have them do to you; for this is the law and the prophets" (Matt. 7:12). If there is a division among peoples, they are to be reconciled with one another before going to the altar to offer their gifts to God (Matt. 5:24). Jesus' table fellowship with the social outcasts, viewed as sinners, proclaims the message of forgiveness and reconciliation for those who follow the way of God. Yet many Christians find problems in forgiving others and in being forgiven.

Being able to receive God's forgiveness and to participate in forgiving/reconciling relationships often connects with one's self-identity learned within family and society. John Patton in *Is Human Forgiveness Possible?* perceives shame as the context for dealing with issues of human forgiveness. An emphasis on feelings of guilt for specific sins and specific actions neglects the problem of shame and a person's vulnerability to one's true self in being able to forgive and to receive forgiveness.

As discussed in the previous chapter, guilt is a powerful force in reinforcing unhealthy shame in which one is caught in an unrelenting cycle of living with shame. When persons focus solely on guilt for actions and struggle in receiving forgiveness from God or others and in giving and receiving forgiveness within human relationships, the real problem may be in one's shame-based self-identity. To become aware of guilt and the possibility of forgiveness leading to true reconciliation and freedom to love, individuals must deal with their sense of shame.

Christian traditions of sacramental reconciliation and forgiveness of sin that deemphasize shame in order to emphasize guilt may offer a forgiveness that is more associated with excusing that lacks the possibility of the depth of forgiveness. A person who experiences being excused and not being taken seriously as sinner (specific act done or attitude held) by parents, friends, or spiritual companion may not believe in the possibility of reconciliation and restoration of broken relationships; a person is not called out of the hiding place of shame-based identity into one's true self.

When not taken seriously, individuals are reinforced in their shame in the message that what they do does not really matter. They feel initially a sense of relief, yet in the long run, they think, *Once they truly find out about me, they will not love me.* Instead of growing in discretionary shame, persons grow more deeply into unhealthy shame. "Our forgiveness and the possibility of forgiving . . . are to be found in the context of the question: 'Adam, where art thou?' But we can find forgiving in ourselves only when we discover our relationship to one who calls us out of our hiding places."[3]

The parable of the prodigal (Luke 15:11–32) is about establishing the possibility of forgiveness and reconciliation. The prodigal, aware of his sinfulness and sense of unworthiness, instructs his father to treat him like one of the hired servants. He sees himself as sinner having no value in relating as son to father. Yet the father, pained deeply by his son's squandering, makes reconciliation possible in relating to him realistically. In effect, the father says, "You are not a hired servant. You are my son."

William Oglesby reflects on the scriptural story of Cain and Abel as illustrative of persons who present behaviors of conformity (Cain) or rebellion (Abel) as facades to their true selves and thus are shielded from experiences of forgiveness.[4] While shame may be the basis of such behaviors, a brief discussion will provide the spiritual companion with added insights. The conformist, like Cain, can obscure one's need for forgiveness in going along with life rather than living within the pressures of existence. In conforming, the Cain-person loses the opportunity to deal constructively with failure and misses the creative, though sometimes painful, experience of being forgiven. This person often suffers spiritually in being excused (because of good conformity) and, therefore, does not experience being truly loved through forgiveness.

The conformist spiritual seeker discovers forgiveness through the spiritual companion's honesty. For example, "What you did was destructive and you must bear the consequences. I want to help bear this burden with you. Who you are means more to me than what you did." Through her loving honesty, the companion walks with the seeker in his growing openness to his true self before God, self, and others.

Abel, the rebellious one, represents those who behave in atypical (and sometimes destructive) ways in gaining attention and often have difficulty in dealing with success or with seeing the self as valuable. Abel-persons mask their need for forgiveness by standing alone and rebel against external demands in gaining attention. Abel-persons may also be those who need to be right or righteous as a substitute for the pain of not being loved; they may withhold forgiveness as a defense against further inner hurt and pain. Their anger at not feeling loved becomes a punishment for others in withholding forgiveness. They hide their true feelings because "people don't want to hear about me." Or they think, *No one loves me enough to forgive me.*

The Abel-seeker may struggle with seeing himself as standing with a group within community. He may desire others to engage the community on his behalf. The spiritual companion can assist in liberating the seeker from behind his shield by joining him in his struggle. "I don't know about other people, but I do know I am very much interested in how it really is for you." "I stand with you, not instead of you, and together we can find strength."

Human forgiveness is necessary in all committed relationships. Depending upon the inner resources for faithfulness and courageous love of those involved to bear debilitating circumstances, forgiveness mobilizes the human spirit. By introducing forgiveness into the relationship, persons can prevent or reverse the direction of breaking their commitments.

Without forgiveness within any committed relationship, there is generally no possibility for long-term commitment. While true impossibility can release one from the relationship, the notion of impossibility must not be considered a kind of "cheap grace." A decision of impossibility of reconciliation is a difficult decision to make and a decision that should not be taken lightly. The point of impossibility is the point beyond which one is unable, physically, psychologically, or morally, to go or at least unable to continue in the committed relationship without terrible destruction to oneself and others.

For example, a relationship of sexual, physical, or emotional abuse makes it impossible for the abused to remain without repentance (which includes ceasing the abuse) of the abuser and true forgiveness sought and given. Marital partners may seek to open up possibilities within their struggling marriage through reframing or reinterpreting their relationship. Yet if, for example, one partner is ultimately unable to forgive the other for temporary unfaithfulness, the possibility for continued committed relationship is lost.

The inability to forgive within committed relationships may be associated with a person's inability to work through the anger in being hurt by the one loved. Anger is often considered to be an unacceptable emotion, or one fears expressing the anger inappropriately. Anger, properly understood, is a response to a threat of one's personhood or to something significant in one's life. Feeling the anger and expressing it appropriately indicate caring about oneself, about the relationship, or about what is being threatened. Anger withheld or suppressed limits the energy necessary within a relationship for two people to move toward forgiveness.

Withholding the energy of anger, a person is more likely to respond by dumping blame, demanding the other to satisfy one's ego, and getting stuck emotionally in the relationship. There exists within the relationship an unknown (what is truly threatened) to which the committed persons cannot directly respond; a win-lose dynamic may be set up in which forgiveness is impossible.

Releasing the anger energy addresses the threat and makes room for the energy necessary for forgiveness. Expression of anger relative to what is threatened turns the hurt from within a person and opens the way for the individuals to deal realistically with their situation. Expression of anger gives the other an opportunity to provide more information about the event that was hurtful and opens the door for both parties to validate each other's position. The expression of anger is a doorway through which persons in a committed relationship can move toward forgiveness of oneself and each other.

To imitate God's forgiveness, one must first discover the depth of healing of one's own sinfulness and forgiveness. The parable of the unforgiving servant in Matthew 18:23–35 is illustrative of one who has not fully discovered divine forgiveness of sin and is, therefore, unable to forgive others. The reign of God is like the reign of a king who freed his pleading servant of his debts and who expected that servant to forgive the debts of his co-servants. The servant, having not grasped the forgiveness of his own debts, was unable to forgive the debts of others. "Should you not have had mercy on your fellow servant, as I had mercy on you?" (Matt. 18:33).

Spiritual Companioning

The task of Christian spiritual companioning is to assist the seeker in recognizing his sinfulness, in being strengthened in faith in God's covenanted love of forgiveness, and in growing in imitation of God's actions of forgiveness.

The companion must be aware of sin and forgiveness in her own life and in the life of the seeker; she listens from a stance of being in a world of grace and a world of sin.

The spiritual companion examines her responses to the seeker and avoids the tendency to excuse or to dismiss the reality of sin and the masks of forgiveness. She is open to invite the seeker to name the shame, anger, conformity, or self-righteousness, and to discover his motivations in relation to God's love and freedom.

The spiritual companion takes seriously the seeker without giving in to the "cheap grace" of passing over sin and the need for forgiveness. In being unafraid of naming sin in an honest and caring manner, the companion offers the seeker the possibility of moving toward the experience of God's care and forgiveness that becomes transformative for him. Her praying sincerely at the beginning of the session that includes the desire not to be blocked through her sinfulness and to be open to the seeker's innermost goodness can enable the companion to listen more realistically.

The spiritual companion gently guides the seeker to examine his primary orientation in life as discovered through particular experiences. "Are you aware of the motivation that led you to (this or that action)?" "What might God say to you now (in this situation or this action)?"

The companion is attentive to body and verbal language as the seeker interacts with her. A seeker who looks down when speaking of a wrong that he did, switches topics when she raises questions about his part in difficult relationships, or is unwilling to let go of anger at being wronged may be telling her of an underlying shame or threat that is blocking him. She can help him unmask this through her care and invitation. "I noticed that when you shared (this or that), you looked down. Are you feeling ashamed right now?" "I am aware of your strong anger the last few times we have met. I am wondering if you are able to identify what threat this situation presents to you?"

Exploring with the seeker his image of God can also bring to light his sense of self in relation to God. She then further guides the seeker by her acceptance and working with his image. "When you think of God as judging you right now, what is that like for you?" She may offer the seeker a scriptural passage (the prodigal, the woman who lost her coin) to pray with before the judging God.

The companion can also utilize a human situation of forgiveness that the seeker has had or share a story from her own life of being forgiven that will facilitate the seeker's openness to being forgiven. "I recall when I was young and stole from my parents. I was frightened because I wasn't who I was supposed to be, and I knew my parents would be very angry. It took me a long time to confess it to them. Once I did, though, my mom said, 'Your father and I knew that. We were just waiting for you to tell us.' My fear and underestimation of my parents' ability to forgive left me stirred up for weeks. Is this similar to what you're experiencing now in relation to God?"

To assist the seeker in coming to an awareness of who he is in his life of grace and freedom, the companion may suggest the daily exercise of examen, or review of one's day. This examen involves five steps. First, one asks for God's light of understanding. Second, one reviews the day in thanksgiving, walking through the day, place to place, person to person, thanking God for everything. Third, one reviews feelings that surfaced throughout the day. Fourth, one focuses on one of the feelings (positive or negative) and expresses a prayer that arises spontaneously. Fifth, in looking toward the next day, one focuses on any feeling that surfaces and turns it into prayer. Closing the exercise can be the Prayer of Jesus or another prayer that is important for the individual.[5]

Questions for Reflection

1. What is your understanding of sin and forgiveness?
2. How do you experience yourself as one who sins? Who forgives?
3. What specific experiences have you had of being forgiven? By God and by others?
4. How do you experience yourself as a forgiving person?
5. What is your particular pattern of hiding?
6. What scriptural reference cited in this chapter has particular significance for you? What makes it significant?
7. How is God speaking to you at this time? Do you have any response to God's word(s) to you? Would the daily practice of examen be good for you?

Take some time to pray with one of the scriptural passages cited in this chapter. Perhaps use the one that you sense would be the more challenging one. At another period of time, pray through the method of focusing. This method is best done with another person who facilitates the steps (i.e., guiding you at each period, which frees you to attend to your own bodily knowing and to let go of thinking through the process). If you are in a group learning process, ask the facilitator or another member to assist you. See Appendix A for this method.

chapter 10

Grief

G rief is the response of one's whole self or total personality to the experience of a meaningful loss. Grief is not something that one gets over, ignores, or defends against. Rather, grief is a process that one grows through in allowing it to become part of one's human experiences and bringing it into all of who one is. Grief is a necessary part of the experiences of loss that requires one's energy and attention over a period of time. In doing his grief work, the spiritual seeker reconstructs his life in a way that transforms him in grief's healing and integrative power.

Grief work is not easy work. One must embrace the pain associated with the loss and live in trust and hope of divine activity present even when one often feels alone and isolated. Hanging onto grief affects a person in many ways, not the least of which is chronic illness. Though healing through the process of grieving is within the individual, the seeker needs another to help draw out the healing. Many people do not heal from loss, not because they do not want to but because they lack the language for what they feel or do not have a safe place to express their grief. Others may have an unrealistic concept about the meaning of strength that inhibits their entering into the process of grief.

The spiritual companion is a major resource in the seeker's grief work. Through her ability to listen compassionately and to encourage the seeker to attend to his grieving, the spiritual companion respects the person and offers him hope in the midst of his pain. The companion's ability, over a period of time, to name losses that she hears in the life of the seeker, to invite him to tell his story of the significance of the loss(es), and to remain with him as he shares his feelings empowers the seeker to discover an inner healing. In being with the seeker as he grows in attending to the work of grief, the spiritual companion must be vulnerable to pain and have a tolerance for sadness and powerlessness. To enter into the process of grieving with another is to companion one on the holy ground of one's deepest and wounded self.

Loss and Grief

All persons, from the beginning of life to death, invest energy in persons, places, and things that leads to the formation of bonds or attachments that nourish and sustain their lives. Initial attachments are made with parents or significant adults in the lives of children. Through these early bonds, children learn of their worthiness in being helped by others and of their ability to cope with difficult, painful experiences.

Adequate parenting or other adult interaction provides children with a sense of trust, connection, and worthiness that sustains them in letting go of certain attachments and reinvesting energy in new persons and objects. Children who, in times of need, have experienced adult anxiety or tenuousness in response to them do not learn that others are there with them in difficult times; they are taught not to count on others.

These children often learn coping skills that are inadequate in nurturing their emotional needs. As they grow into adulthood, these persons invest energy in other relationships that enable them to build life-giving attachments missing in childhood. This new relationship may be discovered at any time yet may come to light in their relationship with a spiritual companion who is able to be present with them in their experience of loss and expression of grief.

When a significant bond one has with a person, place, or thing is broken through death or other causes that sever attachments, a person feels an emptiness likened to starvation in that what one has fed on for healthy nourishment and nutrition is no longer available as it once was. The individual feels some anxiety and an emotional protest in response to the stress created by the severance of the bond; in feeling emotionally starved, one normally feels anxious and wants to fight back for survival.

The experience of detachment activates the feelings, perceptions, and behaviors developed in adult life and those feelings, perceptions, and behaviors developed in early childhood that were never integrated within the adult self; loss stirs the adult self and the inner child of the adult in the adapting to the loss of attachment. Loss is the source of grief in which one is emotionally wounded and is in need of healing. Healing occurs as one divests of the bonding energy placed in the person, place, or thing now gone, adapts to living without what is lost, and reinvests one's energy in new attachments. Feeling and expressing the pain of detachment enable the person to move into a period of adaptation and on to finding new energy to invest in forming significant bonds necessary for living.

Several factors influence the extent or depth of one's felt starvation or grief experience caused by loss. Some factors influencing grief are cultural mores; gender messages; the number and significance of losses in a period of time; the significance of the loss in terms of associated losses; and one's religious belief system. The Indian culture, for example, views the loss of a child through miscarriage or spontaneous abortion as equivalent with the loss of self. A homophobic culture perceives loss of one through HIV/AIDS as a deserved punishment. An example of a gender message affecting the impact of one's loss is the importance given to male identity as a caretaker. The loss of a job for a male can impact his very self-identity and meaning as a provider.

Another factor influencing the depth of grief is the significance to the individual of what was lost. The significance of what was lost is particular to each person; what holds important meaning for one person may be of lesser importance to another. Losing a cancerous leg may be felt more deeply by a woman who is a runner than by a nonrunner. The death of an elderly and ailing spouse may bring a sense of relief that the person is no longer suffering, which lessens the grief one feels in losing a loved one.

Secondary losses experienced through a primary loss affect one's grieving by adding additional stress and detachments. For example, a person who loses a partner may also lose financial security, adequate housing (based on the previous income of the partner), socialization built around being a couple (the person is no longer part of a couple and loses identity), and one's best friend. If the loss of a person is the result of a violent act (murder, beating, heart attack after being robbed), the loss is compounded by the loss of an ideal and hope that people care for one another. Several losses, then, multiply the experience associated with the loss of a partner.

The role of one's religious belief system is another major factor in the effect of loss. A person who becomes disabled from degenerative arthritis and believes that it is a punishment from God will be more deeply affected in one's self-concept than the person who believes that God is caring and able to comfort in times of physical pain and suffering. A Christian's belief that all of human life is a movement toward eternal life in God can lessen the grief resulting from the loss of a parent through death; it may also help a person respond to profound questions raised at the untimely death of a child or of one through violence.

As these examples illustrate, there are different categories or kinds of losses that precipitate grief. The most profound loss is the loss of a significant person. The loss of a loved one through death, divorce, separation, or the loss of significant persons necessary for one's life is felt deeply within human beings. Persons who are abandoned or abused emotionally, physically, or sexually as children experience a loss of having had the "right set" of parents to nurture, guide, protect, and care adequately for them in childhood. Some experience a loss in not having the "right kind" of faith leaders if they experienced abuse by clergy or religious leaders. Grief precipitated by the loss of a significant person is that of primary attachments.

A second category of loss is the loss of an aspect of oneself—loss of esteem, limb, faith, security, ability to express oneself, being single, eyesight, hearing, sexual ability, or health. Persons challenged with mental illness or physical disabilities often experience the loss of not fitting into the social norm of appropriate behavior. The grief from such losses may be the grief of powerlessness, imperfection, or meaninglessness.

A third kind of loss is the loss of external objects such as prized possessions, animal or pet, home, or car. Associated with this loss is the grief of having lost safety or security if one has been robbed or experienced other acts of violence, including the minimization of one's loss.

A fourth category is that of developmental loss. The most common loss is the loss associated with the maturation process in which one loses who one was and becomes another (e.g., adolescence to adulthood, middle-aged to elder). Other developmental losses occur at marriage, religious commitment, or other personal commitments. One loses one's position in life, and there is a shift in the degree of dependence, independence, and interdependence.

These losses are inevitable, and the grief may go unnoticed and unattended to when associated with the positive choices one makes in growing into adulthood. For example, if one marries, there is the loss of being single, of being detached from a certain degree of independence. Not recognizing what one gave up in choosing a good, a person may delay one's grief that is later expressed inappropriately; a person's chronic blame of one's partner may be the misplaced emotions related to unresolved grief in losing a single lifestyle. When longing for the realities of previous times in life, a person may need to attend to the grief work of letting go of those times in order to invest energy in the present situation. Losses are a normal part of living and are uniquely experienced by each individual. The depth of a person's grief is directly related to the significance of the loss and its impact on the individual.

The role of the spiritual companion is to listen and to help the seeker articulate what the loss means to him. She also assists the seeker in naming his experiences over a period of time. For example, a seeker dealing with a loss that has minor significance for him may wonder why it is having a major impact on him. The companion, remembering other events in his life, may recognize that this is his fourth loss in less than two years. She helps him by naming what he has been through. "I hear that this loss is not a major one for you, yet I am aware that in a short period of time you have lost your parent, have moved into midlife, and have become an 'empty nester.' You have hardly had time to heal emotionally from one loss before another comes along." Using her fingers to count off the losses helps the seeker visually see the burden of losses in his life.

Or the seeker may be sharing his decision to leave a job in which he has been unhappy. While affirming his decision to leave the job and to seek another, the companion will eventually want to raise for the seeker the question of what he will be giving up in leaving. This question of "What will you have to let go of in leaving your job?"—though not dealt with immediately—helps the seeker name his losses in the midst of his positive decision. Another way the companion can help the seeker to attend to his grieving is to ask,

"What will you take with you, and what will you leave behind from this job experience?" An exercise is for the seeker to image putting what he wants to take in a suitcase and throwing the other things away.

Specific Grief

In attending to issues of loss and grief, it is necessary to identify very specific types of grief: anticipatory, sudden or traumatic, no-end, near-miss, inhibitory, and pathological grief.

- Anticipatory grief is the emotional response one feels in anticipation of loss. Such grief is felt in anticipation of a job layoff, of loss of a loved one who has a terminal illness, of surgery for an amputation, of total loss of eyesight, hearing, or one's capacity through Alzheimer's disease.
- Traumatic or sudden grief occurs when loss happens through traumatic events such as sexual abuse or rape, accidents, fires or floods, the loss of a child through SIDS (sudden infant death syndrome), or the death of one through murder.
- No-end grief is felt when there are constant reminders of the loss, such as with divorce when one is in contact with (or hears about) one's partner or children after the loss of the marriage, with chronic illness or amputation of breast or limb in which one is reminded physically or visually of the loss on a regular basis, and with abuses from church personnel that one is reminded of when seeing church buildings.
- Near-miss grief is the emotional response to the realization "It could have been me." Survivors of war, siblings of children who were abused, family members of those with alcoholism or other addictions, and persons behind a car involved in a tragic accident deal with near-miss grief.
- Inhibitory (or delayed) grief occurs when persons temporarily shut off their emotions or exhibit an inability to recognize loss. Inhibitory or delayed grief may result from normal shock or numbness, from an effort to get through a crisis period, or from a belief in the false myth that to experience pain one will go crazy.
- Chronic or pathological grief is a state of permanent avoidance of the process of grief in which persons deny their experiences of loss and/or their responses to loss. In this permanent state of denial or avoidance, these persons may be led to abuse drugs, alcohol, or sex, or to attempt other self-destructive behaviors including suicide. Those who demonstrate either inhibitory or pathological grief ought to be referred to and encouraged to seek professional psychological care.

Grief Indicators

As an emotional response of one's total self to loss, grief is made manifest in changes in one's usual physical, behavioral, affective, social, cognitive, and spiritual being. The degree to which grief manifests itself is relative to each person's reality. There are any number of reactions to grief, but there are no right or wrong ways. A person may react in one of the ways or in more than one way.

Knowing how the personality responds to grief helps the spiritual companion to normalize the seeker's unusual feelings, thoughts, and actions. There are times in which a spiritual seeker is unaware of his need to grieve, yet he shows signs associated with the experience of significant loss. A seeker may be carrying unresolved grief from immediate loss or from past losses that he was never able to work through. Being aware of some of the ways in which grief manifests itself, the spiritual companion can explore with the seeker the possibility of his grieving and open the door for him to engage in the healing work of grief.

Some physical and behavioral manifestations of grief are shortness of breath, dry mouth, stomach or back pains, intestinal or bladder difficulties, pulse or blood pressure increases or decreases, insomnia, headaches or muscle tensions, nightmares, dizziness or lightheadedness, changes in menstrual cycle, weight gain or loss, tiredness, tearfulness, altered voice or speech pattern, bodily weakness (especially in the legs), sweaty palms, and changes in appetite, appearance, sleep habits, sexuality, or body posture. In walking with the seeker through present or unresolved grief, the spiritual companion does not ignore his need for medical intervention when appropriate. One who has a prolonged shortness of breath or heart palpitations (over several days), for example, needs to seek medical care to rule out physical health problems. The spiritual companion's task is to be attentive to the issues of loss and grief and to encourage the seeker to obtain the proper care he needs from other caregivers.

Affective and social indicators of grief are noticed in a seeker's emotions and styles of interacting that are not common for him. For example, a person who generally feels happy now feels sad, angry, and/or anxious. A person with a steady or calm personality may feel restless or agitated. Feelings of anger, blame, guilt, jealousy, suspicion, low self-esteem, worthlessness, and fear are also normal for persons in grief.

Depression is sometimes an indicator of an inability to name or to feel sadness or anger; one depresses feelings that are considered inappropriate or too risky to feel. Socially, a person may become irritable, withdrawn, moody, or overly self-critical. Lacking the initiative and one's general interest in things and people is often experienced by the person in grief.

The spiritual companion can help by normalizing these feelings for the concerned and grieving seeker. "I hear how difficult it is for you to feel sad and angry. These are normal feelings for anyone grieving. Your surgery was a major loss." It is important for the spiritual companion to be with the seeker in his feelings and to attend to how he might be acting out of these feelings. "Do you care to say more about your anger?" "What are you doing with your feelings of guilt?" "Would it be helpful for you to share more about it with me?" "What do you think you need to know to help you through this part of your grief?" The companion also notices any changes in the seeker that he may not have identified. "I noticed that you look sad today. Are you feeling sad?"

Loss and grief also bring about dissonance in one's intellectual or cognitive functioning. One may be less able to concentrate on details, be forgetful and inattentive, have mental blocks, and make errors in judgment (e.g., in distance). The grieving person may worry more than usual, be preoccupied more often, and be unaware of external reality. The seeker may need to have these functional changes normalized by the spiritual companion. He may also need to be helped in making a realistic plan or goal for himself that is within his abilities at this time. For example, if a seeker is concerned that the inability to concentrate is affecting his job performance (a job he does not need to lose in addition to the loss already experienced), the companion may ask him, "What do you think would be a helpful way for you to remember things?" or "Could you ask any people around your workplace to help you remember things?"

The particularity of grief for each person makes it impossible for another to grasp fully an individual's inner responses. Even when the companion has had the same loss (death of a parent, loss of a child, divorce, loss of midlife to elder years), she cannot fully comprehend the impact on the seeker's spirit.

All of the above mentioned indicators or personality reactions to loss and grief affect the inner life of the seeker. In addition, the person of faith whose relationship with God was as co-creator may experience a greater need for dependency on God or be unable to discover the presence of God in the midst of the pain and suffering of loss and grief. Another person may find his spirit is lifted up by a God who is there without his having to feel God's presence. A shift in how one has viewed and experienced his God-relationship may occur, or one may draw more upon that relationship.

The attentive companion will ask, "Where is God in the midst of your pain?" or "Does God care about the pain?" A seeker, never before having viewed God as Someone to be angry with, now feels angry at God for not taking care of him. A spiritual companion can gently foster the seeker's expression of this anger to God.

Grief Work

Grief work is the spiritual movement of letting go and living on; it is an inner journey of transformation in the face of loss. Grief work is the process of meaning making in which an individual experiences a significant detachment, works through divesting of the bonding energy, adapts to reality in the absence of what has been lost, and reinvests in new attachments. Grief work is the work of healing the wounds created by loss. It involves the experience of loss and the expression of emotions connected to the distress of detachment. Both experience and expression are key elements in the process of grieving. Ignoring their losses, persons minimize their experiences and thwart going deeper into themselves; they prevent the possibility of spiritual transformation in becoming more of who they are.

When the emotions precipitated by the experience of loss go unexpressed, they take up energy space within the individual and serve as inner "clots" that block further attachments; unexpressed emotions take up the inner energy necessary for healthy relationships that one needs for life. Not expressing one's emotions is like plugging up a vital feeding tube in one's inner life. Release of emotions in doing the work of grief allows the person (body, mind, emotions, spirit) to integrate what was lost into one's reality and to make room emotionally for fuller living.

The first task of grief work is to experience and accept the reality of loss. In the face of loss, a person may be in shock or denial and feel afraid. These initial responses are positive in that shock, denial, and fear are ways that a person initially protects the self from the felt starvation that loss brings about. These responses often provide a person with the necessary time to find oneself in the midst of the loss and to avoid a state of panic in which one becomes closed to others and to his own inner resources. A person may express his shock, denial, or fear in different ways—crying, seeking solitude, withdrawing, clinging, being busy—depending on cultural, social, and gender needs. Individuals will articulate feeling numb, splattered all over, lifeless, empty, lost in a barren desert. These responses and articulated feelings describe the initial effects of detachment; persons experience a sense of being in an uninhabited, uncultivated inner wilderness. Only when these responses remain for an extended period of time do they become dangerous to the health of the individual.

In her ability to journey with the seeker the companion sets the environment of trust within which the seeker can enter into the work of grief. The companion's awareness of her assumptions about responses to loss is necessary as she remains nonjudgmental and compassionate. For example, if the companion assumes women cry and men do not cry, she may respond with surprise (or be shocked) when a man cries, or she may push the more task-oriented woman to cry. If she is familiar with the wilderness and its need for slow and careful cultivation to be able to produce life, the companion will be a nourishing presence in receiving the person as he presents himself.

Some persons are unable to experience or accept loss because of a negative self-concept in which they perceive themselves as unworthy of relational bonds or because they are incapable emotionally to form intimate relationships. Unresolved issues of fear, trust, shame, or guilt acquired in relationship with one's parents as a child or in later abusive relational situations can block a person from forming healthy attachments.

Persons unable to establish healthy attachments because of a fear of abandonment perceive themselves as not having the outer or inner resources necessary to cope with the stress of loss. They have not integrated within their life experiences the health and value of attachments and the nurturing strength that can sustain them in times of loss. Therefore, a denial of a present loss may be more than normal self-protection. Denial of loss may be the denial of one's human need for intimacy, connection, and trusting relationships. A protest such as "I exist alone!" or "I need no one and nothing!" or "I am my own person!" or "People and things mean nothing to me!" may be an emotional protest to an earlier loss of trust or a protest against having been taught one is of no value.

A seeker's response to an apparent loss may indicate his need for growth around a more accurate self-concept. This latter growth is, indeed, a form of grief work in letting go of the old/false self-identity and moving toward the integration of the self. The companion who listens empathically can hear the cry and feel the masked pain of the seeker. She will let go of guiding the seeker through grief work focused on the present loss and gently invite him to enter into the grief of earlier losses.

The companion may want to use herself in such an invitation. For example, "I feel sad as I think about you having to go it alone. In fact, I feel scared. Do you ever feel that way?" In this approach the companion invites by connecting through care and compassion with the seeker. Such connection can enable the seeker to name his woundedness and to trust that the companion relationship can help him discover healing.

Storytelling interspersed with periods of silence and with the performance of tasks enables the person to move from the place of desert, numbness, denial to the place of acceptance of the loss. Recounting the events of the loss multiple times helps the personality incorporate the truth of what happened; telling the story helps one to believe the reality of loss. Periods of silence allow the whole self to realize subconsciously that loss has occurred and life is changed. Performance of tasks (including physical exercise) helps persons to "work out" the numbness or shock and to rediscover a capacity for energy that has been stripped from them in the loss. The "percentage" or balance of storytelling, silence, and tasks will depend on the person and the circumstances of one's grief. It is important, however, that all three are part of the seeker's early grief work in experiencing and accepting the reality of loss.

The spiritual companion can provide openers for the seeker by asking leading questions. "What happened?" "Where were you when you heard the news?" "What do you want?" "What needs do you have right now?" "Are you finding enough time to be silent when you need to?" "Are you able to take care of necessary tasks?" These same questions may need to be raised in more than one session as the seeker tries to accept the reality of loss. By her calm presence and consistency in listening, the companion assures the seeker of the manageability of his grief work.

The companion's use of reflective listening in response to the seeker is effective in the naming of loss for those unable to identify their experience as well as for those trying to accept loss as a reality. For example, the companion may note, "As I listen to your experiences, it sounds as though you do not receive positive feedback that is important to you in feeling energized at work. That is quite a loss." "Losing a parent is very difficult." "It is hard to realize that you have lost a sense of immortality in having cancer." The companion's patience in initiating openers; encouragement of the seeker to tell the story, to spend time in silence, and to do what he needs to do; and presence in listening provide the seeker permission to do his grief work. She is also letting the seeker know that she honors his pace in the grief process.

In coming to terms with the reality of loss, the seeker may struggle with how God could have allowed loss to happen. Believing in a God of care and protection, the grieving person may experience the absence of God as he feels confused, alone, and hungry for affection and safety. "Where is God?" "This couldn't be true if there is a God." The spiritual companion reverences the seeker in his attempt to make sense of his experience by affirming him as a person with these concerns; she does not try to theologize or interpret God. "Those are very good questions. I might be asking the same questions if I were you. You must feel very alone and confused." Such a response, at the appropriate time, from the companion assists the seeker in naming his feelings that are being protected by denial or shock. She may invite the seeker to ask God these questions. "Do you think you can ask God where God is or who God is at this time?" The companion, with the permission of the seeker, can also include his questions in prayer at the end of the session.

As one accepts the reality of loss, the grieving person no longer experiences a numbness. From a sense of being in a barren place, the individual is filled with the emotions of protest associated with the significance of the loss. The healing process of grief work now entails the expression of feelings, the divestiture of one's bonded energy to what is no more.

This expression of feelings is often considered the "core of grief" work yet should not be isolated from the acceptance of the reality of loss. It is not a time for resolving the pain; it is a time for sharing the energy of the pain by naming one's feelings with another. The companion enters into the pain of the grieving person by her encouraging the seeker to articulate his feelings. Her calm reception of whatever feelings are expressed (and in whatever appropriate way they are expressed) lets the seeker know of his goodness and the value of his feelings.

The focus of the companion should be more on the seeker's process than on delving into the content. The companion listens lovingly as the seeker talks through and expresses his feelings until they gradually are released. Depending on the depth of one's grief, a person may not experience such release for several months. The companion's ability to tolerate unrelenting pain with the seeker enables her to lighten the seeker's burden by carrying the yoke of pain with him. Both the seeker and the companion engage in a period of profound vulnerability in which the companion is like a midwife of the seeker's emotions. The companion does not let the person's pain frighten her; she remains in the pain, knowing that healing is occurring in the release of the emotional energy.

This phase of the grief work cannot be rushed, excused, or explained. It continues the meaning making of life in the face of loss. Too often a person hears, from those unable to manage or tolerate pain because they cannot "fix it," that one ought to get on with life. "You have to get over this." Or one's loss is overly spiritualized in order to avoid the pain. "God loves those who suffer. You must be very blessed at this time." Thus, the companion needs to be able to hear the person's pain as a movement in the process of letting go in order to live on. Signs of depression or interference with routine (see the section on grief indicators) may point to the person's need of other assistance yet does not take away the importance of the companion being with the grieving seeker.

The seeker's emotional release occurs in his direct expression of feelings, in his verbalizing of self-concept/image, in his behaviors, and in his feelings, thoughts, and images of his relationship with God. "How can I be so stupid to have left the house?" is an expression of self-anger and self-blame in being responsible for the loss of the house by fire. "My God, my God, where are you? Do you even care?" is a cry of anguish in the midst of aloneness. "I can't go on without my wife" expresses the pain of the broken bond of marriage. "Why is this happening to me?" is the pain of feeling unfairly treated. Grief work often taps into a person's sense of justice and one's image of God. "If God is just and rewarding and I am good, how did I lose my leg?"

The companion affirms the pain and makes a personal commitment to stay with the person in his pain. She can be of help in asking the seeker to say more about his directly expressed feelings or to name the feelings behind the seeker's behavior and behind his concepts of self and/or God. "Your cry to God is very deep. You must feel very, very far down in a pit." "Your wife meant a great deal to you. You must have lost much in her death."

Silence on the part of the empathic companion can provide a safe and comforting environment for the seeker to express his feelings. The seeker can sense the compassionate energy of the companion who reverences the reality that no words can or should wipe away the pain. Sometimes a companion can image holding or rocking the hurting seeker who is expressing forcefully his feelings (sobbing, crying out, pounding the table) and silently repeating a mantra of care: "I care. I care. I care."

The companion is attentive in not letting the seeker make decisions during this time of pain that will potentially involve other losses. For example, a seeker, grieving the lost of his best friend who moved, may declare, "I will never again get close to anyone." Responding to the pain and yet cautioning the seeker, the companion says, "I understand how you feel right now, yet you will be able to form other friendships and find ways to nurture this friendship in the future."

The release is the letting go in order to make room to live on. Expressing painful feelings does not cause one to go crazy or to do crazy things. In fact, the opposite is generally true. One feels greater freedom, hope, and a sense of manageability of one's life when the release of the pain is appropriately and adequately accomplished with the companionship of another. Letting go occurs when one is able to endure and accept the feelings that accompany the experience of loss and to tolerate the fears, helplessness, and waiting to hope again. The seeker's feelings may be mentioned in prayer at the end of each session as a way of giving them "holy voice." "God, we come to you as we are. We know that you hear and hold lovingly (the seeker's) anger and confusion. Blessed be you and blessed be (the seeker) and me as we walk this painful journey."

The expression of the pain of grief may take weeks or longer to be released. The length of time is associated with the depth of the grief in relation to the significance of the loss, the individual's defenses and coping skills, and the availability of other support resources outside the companion relationship. There are several signposts to indicate that this period of the seeker's grief work is being completed. Some signs that the seeker manifests are as follows: a balance of the positive and the negative in the accounts of a relationship broken by death, divorce, or other cause; an expressed ability to forgive if necessary; a sense of hope; and a lessening of the depth of pain. At this point, the seeker's grief work is the work of adaptation, that is, adjusting to living without what was lost.

Many times in expressing his pain, the grieving person voiced his needs that were lost. Remembering what the seeker expressed, the companion can guide him through the next phase. She must be aware of the seeker's response as she begins the journey into adaptation; the companion may sense the seeker's readiness, yet he is not quite ready for such an adjustment.

The companion does well to remember that the individual's grief work is not linear but cyclical. The work of acceptance of the reality of loss, the expression of the pain, and adaptation can be visualized as a spiral of grief work rather than a linear step-by-step process. For example, as the grieving person taps into the pain of the loss, he becomes more deeply aware of the reality of loss and reenters telling his story surrounding the loss. This, in turn, unearths new pain and a new level of release of the pain. As one begins to make plans, to be less preoccupied with the thoughts and emotions surrounding the pain of loss, and to feel as though one is "over the hump," something may trigger the pain that needs new expression. This latter will probably be less intense yet real and is in need of care.

Adjusting to the environment without what has been lost entails the work of finding meaning, hope, and direction. The grieving person is often self-absorbed in seeking his alternatives for living. Many times persons who have lost a loved one tend temporarily to isolate themselves from others to figure out not only how they can belong but also who they are.

The grieving person, in releasing his invested energy in what was lost, makes room for new relationships. This reinvesting of energy includes the inner conviction that forming new bonds is not replacing the old (that can never be replaced) but creating new ones needed for one's life. For example, a widower is no longer a husband who is a caring and fun-loving person. He is a widower who is caring and fun-loving and changed by his experiences. Forming new relationships as a widower does not replace the bond established with his wife.

The seeker who has had a significant loss has been changed internally in the process of grieving yet may appear the same person externally to others. No one else has entered fully into the seeker's experience; no one else has changed with him as he has changed. In this period of adaptation in the grief process, the seeker continues to be vulnerable before others and God. It is the period of surrender to what was lost as being no more, adapting to life and committing to live on. The seeker is now ready to make life-giving decisions for himself.

The companion is able to recall things that are important for the seeker. By tapping into these things, the seeker is able to make decisions on alternative ways of being nourished. The companion may say, "I recall how important it is for you to listen to others. Now, in the midst of your coworkers giving you a lot of attention since surgery, are there ways you can accept their attention and invite them to share their stories?" Or she may say, "You're right. No one can take the place of your husband. Yet being special is a need we all have. Are there things you can do or other relationships that will help in a small way?" Or she may ask, "What will give you a feeling of life?"

The companion invites the seeker to reflect how God has been present for him through the experience and pain of the loss. "In looking back over this period of grief, how has God been with you?" "Who is God for you now?" "What do you need from God to help you at this time?"

Conclusion

Loss and grief are part of human reality. Enabling the seeker to attend to the work of grief, the companion walks the painful journey with him toward greater freedom and hope. Time itself does not heal all wounds. The work of grief takes time, yet it is what one does in grieving that promotes healing and leads to new hope and freedom. Grief takes time to accept the loss, to let go, to share, to believe, to forgive, to feel good about oneself again, to reinvest energy of attachments. The grieving person needs a reliable, consistent, persevering, and patient companion to walk through the wilderness and into the promised land of hope and freedom.

The seeker, facing broken attachments, needs a person familiar with loss and grief who hopes in the midst of pain and believes that God cares with and for all persons in their human experiences. Grief is a sign of one's capacity to love and to bond in love. Compassionate love will help heal the wounds of loss and enable the seeker to love and experience being loved again and again.

Questions for Reflection

1. Identify three losses in your life. Of what significance was each one? How did you grieve those losses?

2. What were helpful, and what were not helpful, words, actions, or beliefs of others in response to your losses?

3. Who was God for you during your most intense periods of grief?

4. Did the losses and your grief work change your view of yourself and/or of God?

5. Are you able to tolerate pain without having to take it away from others?

6. Is there any unresolved grief in your life? Are you willing to enter into the work of grief with someone at this time?

7. What is your understanding of your role as companion in being with another in loss and grief?

Take some time and pray over your experiences of loss and grief. Pay attention to what wells up within you as you recall your life's journey of loss, grief, and healing. Express your experience in a poem, a journal entry, a picture, or a prayer. Recall any stories in the Hebrew or Christian Scriptures that speak to you of the journey of grief (e.g., the Exodus story, the scene of Jesus in the garden, Mary at the foot of the cross).

chapter 11

Survivors of Abuse

Sexual abuse is a tragic and sad reality of humanity. It affects about one in every three girls and one in every seven boys in North America before the age of eighteen. Sexual abuse affects the emotional, physical, social, and spiritual life of the abused. Because of its consequences to the whole person, sexual abuse has a particular effect on one's spirituality. The adult who reveals a history of sexual abuse to the companion is seeking to heal the spiritual wounds created by the behaviors of others in one's life. The person seeks a life of integration that can be lived more fully and more abundantly. The seeker who has survived sexual abuse is a person of great strength, resiliency, and positive desire to form healthy relationships that were denied him in his formative years.

Healing spiritually from abuse is part of a grief process in which a person moves from perceiving oneself as a victim, to identifying oneself as a survivor, to celebrating and living from a self-concept as victor.[1] In healing spiritually, the seeker breaks through his denial and believes that the abuse happened, experiences the pain of what was lost in being abused, grieves the losses related to it, and learns to trust himself and others in new and vibrant ways. The evil of sexual abuse demands the strength of personal courage and the loving care and hope from others to let go of its power and to engage in living on with a renewed spirit and new energy. The seeker's openness about his history of abuse within the spiritual companion relationship is an occasion for new life. The companion is careful not to too easily spiritualize a history of sexual abuse as a moment of growth.

The role of the spiritual companion with an adult who has been abused is that of nurturer, interpreter, and loving, trusting listener. She is one who can help the seeker break the silence, hear his stories, receive and validate his feelings, and be a living source for the seeker's healing. The companion's role effects a therapeutic healing of the wounded spirit, yet is not to replace the role of professionally trained therapists. It is important, therefore, that the companion have an adequate awareness of sexual abuse, a knowledge of its consequences, and an understanding of how she might be a nurturing companion with those having been abused.

Awareness, knowledge, and understanding enable the companion, who also may have been abused, to be attentive to herself and to her role, including referring the seeker to more trained professional assistance when the seeker's issues and concerns are outside her expertise. When making a referral to a more qualified professional, the companion does not withdraw from the person but maintains her role as one able to participate in a specific way in the healing process. In healing from the experiences of sexual abuse, the seeker deals with many complex issues. The companion serves as a trustworthy advocate in making referrals when necessary and as a loving companion in remaining faithful to her role with the seeker.

Sexual Abuse

Sexual abuse is not about sex or love. Sexual abuse is about power, control, and authority. It is the misuse of the power of an adult-child relationship or the power of the role (parental, counseling, ministerial, companioning) one has in relationship to another. The abuser is in a position of power in which an individual has placed specific trust and confidence. It is a violation of the relationship boundary by sexualizing the relationship.

This sexualizing may be explicit or implicit. Explicit sexualizing includes fondling and oral, genital, or anal intercourse with another. Implicit sexualizing includes certain forms of touching, telling sexual stories or jokes, and performing sex in front of others; it also includes seduction by revealing sexual arousal, deep emotional attachments, or dreams involving the other person. Parental jealousy or insult of the children's friends, parental sickness every time a young adult child plans to go on a date, parental alcoholic seduction, and parental use of sexually suggestive "pet names" (bitch, whore, she dog, slut) for a child are also forms of abuse. This violation of boundaries in a relationship of unequal power (parent to child, counselor to counselee, clergy to parishioner, companion to seeker) inherently controls or manages the affective experiences and diminishes the freedom of the one being abused. The issue of authority in sexual abuse is not that of authoritarianism but of control and management of another's affective life; one's sense of safety and protection, trust, and ability to say no or manage oneself are compromised. Abuse, in effect, is the lying to a child (or other) about the nature of love, safety, and caring.

Sexual abuse occurs within and among all classes, all ethnic groups, all religious traditions, and all sexual orientations. Sexual abuse of children occurs more frequently by those adults known to the children than by those unknown to the victims. Men abuse young girls, women abuse young boys, men abuse young boys, and women abuse young girls. Given the cultural dynamics of power within Western culture, there is a much higher prevalence of men abusing young girls and young boys than women being the perpetrators of abuse. Because of patriarchy and systems of social oppression, sexual abuse is often interlocked with racism, clericalism, and sexism. Thus, healing from the dynamics of sexual abuse may include (or uncover) a complex set of related dynamics from which to grow as victor, as empowered to choose life.

Effects of Childhood Abuse on Adult Life

Childhood sexual abuse is a traumatic event because the event exceeded one's normal coping mechanisms and breaks the primary bond of trust necessary for one to learn how to cope in times of loss. The impact of such a trauma varies, depending on whether the event was a singular or chronic (several times) occurrence, the age of the person when the abuse took place, the existence of other traumatic experiences in the person's life, the occurrence of physical injury associated with the abuse, and the amount of losses experienced or anticipated in one's present life. Adults who were not directly abused and watched a sibling or a parent being abused bear the effects of abuse as bystanders unable to make a difference.

Childhood sexual abuse breaks the important early attachment needs discussed in the previous chapter and precipitates traumatic grief. The child, unable to resolve the loss, carries the effects of the loss and unresolved grief into adulthood. It is important to remember that the effects are being felt now in adult life but the event that precipitated the effects happened in childhood.

The seeker is no longer a victim of the actual abuse; he has survived it. The seeker may still be victimized by the emotional power of the abuse but is now an adult with the capacity to learn to say no to that power. Remembering that the seeker's healing is in letting go of the effects of abuse allows the companion to avoid getting hooked by feeling a personal affront when the seeker's issues of trust enter the relationship.

The companion is free emotionally to become an interpreter for the seeker. For example, a seeker may question whether he can trust that the companion will be on time for the sessions. Instead of feeling hurt or angry that the seeker cannot trust her, she may say, "I know that others you counted on broke that trust for you as a child and you felt insecure. Our relationship is as adults, and I will be here on time. If I am not, I will explain to you what happened that made me late, and I will want to hear how that affects you." This comment by the companion is to be made only *if* the seeker has revealed his history of abuse. The companion ought not to mention abuse or draw the seeker to reveal a history of abuse. Only after trust has been well established ought the companion raise the question about unresolved issues of sexual abuse when the seeker seems stuck in issues associated with abuse.

The companion's approach is done in a way that frees the seeker to reveal sexual abuse or not. For example, the companion may say, "I have experienced you struggling with feeling positive about yourself for a long time. I am wondering if there is anything in your history that would be helpful for you to name that impacted how you feel about yourself—such as alcoholism or other addictions in your family, sexual abuse, or losses that hurt a lot." If the seeker says, "Nothing," or names something else, the companion follows the lead of the seeker.

When abused as children, adult survivors may have been told verbally or intuited emotionally from the abuser that "This is our secret," or "I am doing this because I love you," or "If you tell your mother, it will hurt her." The child, unable to differentiate one's feelings and thoughts, is caught in an emotional trap. The child senses that something is wrong (even when— maybe especially when—sexual penetration may feel good), desires to release these feelings and find out the truth with a trusting adult, yet the child is made to feel responsible for needs of others (mother's hurt, father's need for love) and devalued in one's own needs (keep it a secret).

The message to keep secrets is a powerful one that is frequently carried into adulthood. To break the silence of abuse is to risk hurting others, betraying the adult abuser (from whom one needs love as a child), being isolated and not loved, and being unimportant. The seeker is able to break the silence when he realizes that he has been used by the adult abuser and is able to express his anger at being denied the appropriate parental relationship necessary in his life. The initial anger may be focused toward the parent who did not protect him from the abuser; the seeker's anger is at being betrayed not only by the abuser but also by the nonprotecting parent who did nothing to stop the abuse. One's anger may be at God who is felt to have betrayed the child as well. "Where was God, the Caring Parent, when I was abused?" "God left me alone!" "I prayed and prayed because I thought God cared. Right!" The companion's compassionate reception of the seeker's revelation of abuse and her nonjudgmental listening can assist the seeker in breaking the silence and in letting go of the many dimensions of secrecy in his life. The companion's ability to receive and hear the anger offers the seeker a safe space to move through the anger toward healing.

The abused child becomes conflicted about the meaning of love and intimacy; the time of abuse may be the only time the child gets attention. The sexualization of the relationship in abuse leaves the child, later an adult, with a confused sense of oneself as a sexual being and an inappropriate experience of love and intimacy. Some persons deal with the confusion of sexuality and intimacy by the way they treat their bodies or mask their sexual self through anorexia, bulimia, obesity, or promiscuity.

Some adult survivors seek relationships based on an "all or nothing" mode of relating rather than on the more intimate "both/and" mode of relating. The surviving adult, in an attempt to get one's intimacy needs met, may become enthralled with being affirmed and become overly attached or enmeshed with the affirmer; the adult is all consumed with the other and feels rejected, jealous, or abandoned when the affirmer is not totally available. The adult survivor who is not able to share one's feelings will withdraw from the relationship; the person feels that one gets all or nothing. The companion who maintains a consistency in her relational boundaries and is able to offer an explanation for them can help the seeker learn healthy intimacy.

The companion covenants to be available within the limits of the relationship. Offering an explanation in a caring manner to the seeker wanting more time (socially, by phone, or in meetings) outside the covenant, the companion builds a bridge for the seeker to learn healthy intimacy. She lets him know that he is important, that she cares for him, and that the fulfillment of her needs does not take away his importance or her care. "I know you would like for us to talk on the phone every day. I am not able to do that because of my demands of family and commitments to others. I care about you and what you are going through, and I am committed to being fully available to you in our covenanted time." The companion's care also involves her support for the seeker in his self-care—eating properly, getting sufficient sleep, exercising, playing.

The abused child feels the aggressive power of the abuser and is unable to withdraw physically from the conflict or to resolve it in any other way. In order to survive, the child develops a high level of sensitivity to the moods and feelings of others. Instead of using this sensitivity as a means of establishing intimate relationships, adult survivors of abuse use their sensitivity to avoid conflicts and emotional situations; survivors often work hard to avoid rather than resolve conflicts. In their resilience to survive the emotional (and physical) pain of abuse, children learn that the only way to get their needs met without being abused is through manipulation. Therefore, abused children learn to read every move of others, to recognize others' desires, and to anticipate others' needs before they are stated as a way of pleasing others who, in turn, will be favorable to them in their needs. As adults, they can behave overly responsibly, become workaholics, and communicate indirectly in getting their needs met.

The sensitized seeker, in the presence of the companion, may respond to the companion's questions before she finishes asking them, may answer questions the way he thinks the companion wants them answered, may appear rushed most of the time, and/or may call the companion before each session to verify the time. The companion may naturally feel annoyed, confused about why her questions never get answered directly (even those requiring either a yes or a no). She may feel a desire to control the person by slowing him down or be angry that he is checking up on her each week. However, the companion realizes that she represents a position of power because the relationship is not one of mutual companionship; the seeker is responding as an adult affected by childhood abuse. Her compassion, empathy, and trustworthiness will enable the seeker to trust himself and the relationship.

The companion's use of empathic feedback may be helpful for the seeker to begin to let go of this unconscious and patterned behavior. "I am aware of how sensitive you are in responding to my questions, calling to verify our times, etc. Yet sometimes I feel that this is a real burden on you, a burden you learned earlier in life when life wasn't as safe as it is now. Do you feel this to be a burden? Like always watching over your shoulder?" Or she may say, "Being sensitive is a wonderful gift you have. I would like it not to be a burden for you in our relationship or in any other relationship. Is there some way you can use your gift without its being such a burden for you in adulthood?"

An adult survivor may have internalized shame acquired through the devaluing messages of abuse. The message of worthlessness is, "Whoever one is and whatever one does are not of value unless they fulfill the needs of others." The child's survival depends on noninterference with and assistance in the importance of others. Thus, the child (and later the adult) must hide who one is and what one does; the child (and adult) must become invisible in order to belong in relationship with others.

To protect one's invisibility, the adult may exhibit excessive control of relationships. Appropriate assertion and aggression that enable an adult to set relational boundaries and to protect self from danger are distorted into a form of aggressive control. This control is a safety net that blocks any emotions or personal feelings from entering a relationship; it is self-protection from being known. Such control can be heard in "Whatever you want . . . I don't care," in which a person abrogates oneself and controls by inhibiting a relationship; the other is left alone to decide. Or control may be in the person's need to always have things one's way. The companion can be helpful initially by naming the positive side of the seeker's response and inviting him to share out of his sense of helping another. "I appreciate your concern that I get what I want. That is very thoughtful of you. It would help me, however, to decide if I knew how you felt or thought about. . . . I think you are important and I value your thoughts/feelings." As the seeker finds value in sharing his feelings and discovers personal value in the relationship, the companion nurtures by helping the seeker recognize, affirm, and celebrate his new freedom. "I am aware of your greater spontaneity in expressing your feelings (thoughts). And you do it with such marvelous confidence! Have you noticed that?" "Well, how can we celebrate this?" "Yes, I am open to your letting out one grand whoopee! Can I join you?"

If the abuse occurred at the time of puberty, the child may think that there was something one did to cause the abuse. The child's shame is exacerbated in thinking that the abuse occurred because of something one did to attract the attention or special notice of the abuser. This guilt can protect the abused child's sanity in giving a reason for the abuse, yet it perpetuates the guilt-shame cycle in the adult. The result of such shame messages is that the child grows into adulthood thinking that to "be safe," one must keep a low profile as a way of resolving the guilt feelings.

The adult may struggle with the fear of achieving success, of being noticed in a special way. By helping the seeker to assess realistically his strengths and weaknesses, the companion affirms the seeker's talents and encourages him to use them and not to bury them. The companion may invite the seeker to draw as a prayer exercise a picture of himself (with or without others) as fearful of success and a picture of himself as successful without fear. Together, the seeker and the companion explore what the seeker would need to acquire or let go of to be himself without fear. This exploration may take several sessions. Beginning and ending the sessions with prayers of petition/intercession associated with the seeker's needs will enhance the sacredness of this work.

Young boys sexually abused by their mothers or other adult women whom they trusted often feel an added level of shame because of the cultural messages that men are supposed to be able to protect themselves and that sex with women is romantic and enjoyable. The young boy (or adult) is confused about his male identity as he realizes that he was not able to protect himself and that as a male he did not enjoy the sex of abuse.[2]

Adult survivors, whether abused by women or men, deal with negative myths that say vulnerability is weakness, rigidity is strength, being in charge of one's life is having everything under control, and being comfortable is associated with safety. These myths take on added dimensions in a culture that perpetuates the dominance and power of men. The trauma for young boys and young girls abused by mothers is impacted as well by the cultural norm that moms are more trustworthy than dads. In her care with the adult seeker the companion must consider these cultural factors affecting the trauma of abuse.

Structure can be very difficult for some adult survivors of sexual abuse. The chaotic nature of abuse—lack of boundaries, role shifting/violation, unpredictability of abuse events, physical violence—in which the child was given attention (unhealthy as it was) provides for the abused child a greater affinity for chaos than for structure and order. The child does not learn how to set priorities and to focus one's attention; the familiar is the confusing and chaotic nature of life. A person's unconscious says, "If things are chaotic, then I won't get hurt," or "If they are chaotic, I know what to expect." The abused child learned a certain amount of predictability about chaos.

Moving out of the familiar chaos into structure can be a challenge. Persons (no matter the circumstances) will tend to stay with the familiar rather than choose to move to the unfamiliar; it is natural to cling to what one knows no matter how painful. For a person to change from the familiar, one must give up the familiar and trust that what one does not know is better than what one knows. The companion's provision of structure helps teach the seeker that chaotic behaviors are not necessary in nonabusive relationships; the adult does not need to set up avoidance strategies in the companion relationship.

Spiritual Growth of the Adult Survivor

The spiritual journey of the adult who was sexually abused as a child is the path of moving from bondage to inner freedom and new life. It is the Christian path from loneliness to solitude, from hostility to hospitality, from unmasking the illusions to prayer.[3] The locus of the path is the work of grief. The seeker's spiritual growth involves the following: the reclamation of hope, faith, and trust; the discovery of forgiveness; the incorporation of new images of God; the discernment around the meaning of suffering; and the use of prayer.

The imposed effects of loneliness, isolation, and silence create within the seeker anxiety and fear that can impede his sense of hope of recovery, of faith that his anxieties and fear can be resolved, and of trust in oneself, others, and God. The spiritual journey is that of the grief process in which one experiences the losses of abuse and is able to recover and express suppressed feelings.

In the experience phase of grief work, the Christian survivor is confronted with one's experience of evil and sin and questions not only *what* happened but also *why* it happened. The seeker is faced with the inner struggle of the reality of another's sinful actions causing him pain and suffering. He may also feel a sense of guilt in not being able to say no to the abuse. The companion's ability to affirm that what happened was evil and that no sin of the seeker caused the abuse can be a source of liberation. Her reminding the adult that his feelings of guilt in not saying no may be more associated with his adult capabilities than his ability as a child. The evil that one has experienced must be validated in order for the seeker to find the place of love within himself.

As the seeker accepts the reality of his abuse, his feelings of guilt, shame, anger, betrayal, and abandonment will be released. This phase may also include expression of his confusion with the divine commandment to honor one's father and mother and his need for the companion to interpret accurately the commandment with its expectation of responsible parents. The companion's nondefensive listening to and validation of the seeker's feelings will help him to confront his anxieties and fear, to find the inner power to let go of unrealistic guilt, shame, and fear, and to move beyond the anger to a new personal awareness of who he is. The seeker moves from an identity of victim to one of victor.

The adult survivor discovers forgiveness in the process of the work of grief. The seeker discovers God's forgiveness for his "guilt" in learning why as a child he could not say no. In becoming free of one's identity as a victim, the seeker discovers a sense of forgiveness toward the perpetrator and those (mom, dad, God) who did not protect him.

The seeker discovers that he is open to forgiving abusers. Spiritual growth in the area of forgiveness may include direct forgiveness and reconciliation with abusers who admit sinful actions and repent. Yet the spiritual growth of the seeker resides in his openness to forgive the abusers if ever they came repentant to him. The spiritual companion resists telling the seeker to forgive the abusers "for they knew not what they did." This latter minimizes the impact of the abuse and excuses people who, indeed, know what they are doing. Consequently, such a statement can be interpreted as demeaning of the seeker and his experience. Instead, the companion guides the seeker through the grief process and the discovery of forgiveness.

During his grief work, the seeker may cry out in anger at God: "Why did you allow me to suffer?" or "How could you have done this to me?" or "What do you want from me?" The seeker's anger at God expresses his sense of God's betrayal but also his struggle with the meaning of suffering. The seeker's spiritual movement is to let go of images and meanings that block his healing and to find new images of God and new meaning of suffering within the Christian tradition.

Images of God are formed initially from a child's interaction with parental figures. The image of "an all-powerful Father" or "God as Parent" who loves and protects the Christian can become problematic for an individual abused by a parent. "God did not protect me from abuse. Therefore, God must have approved of the abuse, and I am not included in God's love." "How can Jesus love me and not have stopped the abuse?" God as powerful Father or Parent is not a God with whom the survivor wants a relationship. This kind of God, the child learns from one's parental behaviors, is abusive and excludes the survivor from God's love.

The seeker feels the absence of a personal character of God in relation to him. Some adult survivors have a positive concept of God as Father or Parent. This concept of God enabled the needy child to survive and feel someone cared. Many times, however, these adults do not experience a personal connection with this God. These images of God do not call forth an enlivened response for the person who has been abused. These painful images of God may be surfaced as the companion asks, "Where do you see God in your history?"

The companion can assist by offering scriptural images of God's vulnerability and compassion. In offering these scriptural references, the companion does not defend God but provides the seeker with new images of God that can be life-giving and appropriate. God's vulnerability and compassion point to God's limitations in acting against those who choose to sin and God's loving care and presence with the seeker. God's power is one of suffering love in the midst of human pain, fear, and struggle.

Passages of the Christian Scriptures that illustrate Jesus' solidarity with the weak and vulnerable can be powerful meditations for the seeker in reimaging the Divine in his life. The companion may want to invite the seeker to share what it is like for him to listen to these different images and passages. She may also ask the seeker if reading one of the scriptural passages may be helpful as they begin their time together. Through her gentle guidance, the companion leads the seeker into a new and life-giving connection (reattachment) with God.

The seeker's struggle with the meaning of suffering demands a reconstruction of some Christian interpretations of the crucifixion of Jesus. Theological constructs of the cross grounded in Jesus' atoning for the sins of humankind blur an appropriate meaning of suffering for the survivor of sexual abuse.[4] These theories place God in the position of desiring violent suffering of God's own, Jesus, as a human being. They suggest that God, as a nonoffending parent unable to stop evil, sent Jesus to suffer human violence. They also suggest that children (all human beings) are corrupt until they are saved by God based on suffering.

The implication in these theories for the followers of Jesus is that suffering is a good and something God demands in relation to them. Therefore, the abused can perceive one's suffering as coming from God and intended for the salvation of others; one Child of God (Jesus) gave his life for all other children of God. Or in feeling the guilt of not being able to stop the abuse, the adult hears in these theological theories that he must repent, pledge obedience to God, which is a submissiveness to suffering.

The companion's theological understanding of Jesus' death on the cross as a consequence of his faithfulness to justice in which he confronted the evils of society can enable her to guide the seeker to an accurate understanding of suffering. Jesus, in effect, chose to die on the cross because he chose to live a life directed toward God; Jesus fulfilled the will of God by a life of saying yes to God.[5] Because of the direction of his life, Jesus was a threat to the social powers of his time who devised killing him as a way of getting rid of him. The evil of violence perpetrated upon Jesus was the evil of power against the truth of God's Word. God did not demand Jesus' suffering. Jesus suffered because he was faithful to God in the midst of the social evil of his time. In his suffering, Jesus cried out to God and sought release from the suffering and found God's ever-loving care and embrace. The seeker may find it helpful to dialogue with Jesus, who was faithful and suffered unjustly. During such a dialogue, the seeker may discover Jesus' fidelity in being with him and an ever new sense of God's caring embrace of him.

As the seeker moves through the detachment and adaptation phases of the grief process, prayer is an important component. The companion is attentive, however, in not rushing the prayer life of the seeker or in her using prayer as a substitute (or escape) for her uncomfortable feelings. Some suggestions of the use of prayer have already been made. Techniques of relaxation and centering prayer are particularly helpful. Teaching the seeker the method of sitting quietly, attending to his breath, the expansion and contraction of his body (its aliveness), helps the seeker become aware of his own resource of life. After a period in which the seeker is able to form a rhythm of attentive breathing, he focuses on one word or phrase, repeating it slowly and in rhythm with his breathing. This time of prayer is not to be analyzed; it is to be experienced and integrated into the bodied self of the seeker. To help the integration, the companion may ask, "How was that for you?" or "Is there anything you'd like to share about your prayer experience?" or "How did you experience God during the prayer time or later?"

Ritualizing different movements throughout the grief process is also very important. Rituals of one's Christian tradition can serve in a helpful way. The companion may ask, "Is there any ritual of your faith that would be helpful to you?" For example, some have found reritualizing their baptism is helpful in moving from their victim identity to that of victor. Others find that their participation in the eucharistic celebration in community is a way of affirming their new identity. Blessing with holy water is another restorative and healing ritual familiar to most Christians.

Outside the church's traditional rituals, the companion can offer other rituals to restore and heal the seeker's broken spirit. For example, she can suggest that the seeker draw (or write about) one's anger, guilt, shame, or negative images of God and then ritualize letting go of it by burning the paper, sticking the paper into a container as it burns with the words, "I release you (anger, guilt) from me. I no longer need you. Blessed be my life (body, freed spirit)." Another ritual may be for the seeker to dance or to do other body movement in which he expresses an openness to and reception of the breath of life in the atmosphere. The companion may wish to offer a movement that responds and celebrates the breath of life now shared. Clay, poetry, or music can also be a medium through which one ritualizes an experience. The companion's presence with the seeker during the ritual is an affirmation, a celebration, and offers him a sense of the wider faith community's support.

The Companion's Self-Care

Companioning a person having been traumatized by sexual abuse is a profound grace and an occasion of growth for the companion. Listening attentively and remaining a nonanxious, nonjudgmental presence are not always easy. The nature of violation and the evil of sexual abuse evoke (appropriately) feelings of anger and grief within the justice-minded companion (male or female). If the companion has a history of sexual abuse, her feelings may be from her experience and from her being affected by the seeker's story. The length of time for healing spiritually from sexual abuse means that the spiritual relationship will focus on the consequences (and a renaming of the abuse) for multiple sessions; there is a lingering wound that heals slowly.

The companion needs to take care of herself outside the relationship. Without proper self-care, the companion may find herself colluding with the seeker, becoming anxious that the concerns of the seeker get resolved, feeling overwhelmed, or experiencing fear and anxiety in her life. The companion can become traumatized emotionally without knowing that is what is happening to her.

Taking care of oneself includes having someone to talk with about her feelings, maintaining proper eating, exercise, and prayer, and limiting the number of persons she companions who are growing through their abusive past. The companion's relationship with a consultant or supervisor is especially imperative in order for the companion to be effective and to minimize the potential of being too emotionally affected by the seeker's story.

Conclusion

The spiritual companion relationship is a safe place for the adult survivor to heal from the spiritual wounds of sexual abuse. By her awareness, knowledge, and sensitivity, the Christian companion can be a leaven for the survivor to grow and to live more abundantly. As a Christian, the companion who genuinely cares is reliable, affirms the seeker's dignity and worth, and offers her willingness to suffer with and not problem solve. The companion's ability to listen to the seeker's voice, to acknowledge evil and goodness, to interpret what is truth, and to confront the painful theological interpretations of Christian suffering is healing for the seeker. The spiritual companion relationship becomes a model for healthy relationships in which power is built on care, faithful commitments, and accountability.

Companioning a survivor of sexual abuse is an occasion of spiritual growth for both the seeker and the companion. It is a holy time in which the strength, resiliency, and desire of the seeker for positive relationship with oneself, with others, and with God are nurtured, developed, and celebrated.

Questions for Reflection

1. What is your perception of a person who has been sexually abused?

2. If you have a history of abuse, what are your self-concept and your sense of God?

3. How can God be present with you as you companion someone who has been abused?

4. What is your understanding of suffering? Of Jesus' life, death, and resurrection?

5. How do you care for yourself? Are your body and sexuality important to you? How do you express your sexual self?

6. What more do you need to prepare yourself to companion a person who has been abused?

7. What are the rituals of Christianity that are meaningful to you? In what way(s) are they meaningful?

Do a relaxation exercise concentrating on your body. Choose some music that you like as atmosphere. Go through your body from foot to head, exploring how each part of your body moves and is interconnected with all other parts. Be careful not to leave out the spine, buttocks, or the smallest toe or finger. Pay attention to the feelings that surface for you. What do these feelings tell you about who you are as a bodied person? Imagine yourself standing with God as you are right now. What feelings do you have? What might God be saying to you about your bodied self? Are you able to share this word of God with others or write about it in your journal?

chapter 12

Terminating a Relationship

T he manner in which the spiritual companion relationship ends is as vital a component as the process of beginning. The companion's attentiveness to the dynamics evolved in the early formative stages of the relationship sets the foundation upon which the relationship becomes an effective milieu for the spiritual growth of the seeker. Her attentiveness to the dynamics of termination provides an effective closure to the covenanted relationship in bringing about a sense of completion and resolution to the purpose of the relationship.

The beginning process establishes the covenant upon which the relationship builds and develops for the sake of the spiritual life of the seeker. The ending process affirms the meaning of the covenantal relationship and serves as a bridge in integrating what has occurred and in letting go of the relationship. Appropriate beginning and ending of the spiritual companion relationship affect profoundly (and often unconsciously) the effectiveness of the relationship and the emotional health of the seeker and the companion.

Chapter 1 dealt with the dynamics and issues to be addressed in the beginning process and with the issues involved when the relationship terminates prior to the agreed upon time period. This chapter reviews briefly the reasons for and the elements to be initiated in the process of termination at the end of the covenanted period of the companion relationship.

The Reasons for Terminating

The covenanted relationship between the companion and the seeker has been the key to the spiritual growth of the seeker. At the time of termination, this relationship as it has been is to be discontinued. Termination is more than an ending of the time period; it is the ending of a relationship that brings about a loss for both the seeker and the companion in the way they have been together for a period of time. Therefore, terminating the companionship is bringing to closure the relationship in such a way that both the seeker and the companion can live on without the relationship. The time of termination marks the point of detachment, and the process of closure enables the necessary adaptation (or transition) for the partners to form new attachments and to live on.

An abrupt leave-taking without closure to the relationship thwarts the period of adaptation and can have unhealthy effects on both partners. The seeker may project or transfer onto the next companion (or anyone in a helping role with him) that she must be just like the first companion or just the opposite. The seeker will emotionally look for the attachments he discovered in the nonclosed relationship. He will be hindered initially from entering into a new helping relationship—no matter how much he desires to grow spiritually. The companion may also transfer or project onto other seekers her desire for them to be the extension of this seeker. Her lack of closure inhibits her ability to be a safe, nonjudgmental, and nonanxious presence.

The companion who has not done the work of closure may be tempted to stay in touch with the seeker around issues related to his spiritual life (or any concrete revelation that was part of the companion relationship). Although this may be out of care and a desire to stay connected with the seeker, the companion's initiating of such conversations is generally not appropriate; the seeker has the option of initiating references to the past in future contact with the companion. The companion's connection with the seeker is no longer as it has been. The companion may also feel jealous if she learns that another person is now companioning the seeker. In her jealousy, she may even ask the other companion probing questions about the seeker. This behavior is not appropriate, although the feelings of jealousy and the desire to be connected are normal. The companion's discussion of these feelings with her supervisor or consultant will enable her to grow and continue her development as a spiritual companion. These discussions will also enable her to grow spiritually in letting go and in exploring the meaning of her desires and her jealousy.

In eliminating potential unhealthy aftereffects, the companion's attention to the process of termination has both immediate and long-term positive effects. One immediate effect is that proper closure clarifies and articulates the focus and the context of the seeker's and companion's time together. At the end of the relationship, an articulated reflection of the seeker's concerns, insights, questions, or process during the relationship period helps him to name what has happened and to pull together what he considers important. Closure also helps the seeker (and the companion) to name certain themes or threads that may have surfaced in the spiritual life of the seeker and within the relationship.

A second effect of attending to issues of closure is the elimination of potential misunderstandings between the seeker and the companion. The companion's use of her reflective listening skills at the end of the relationship gives the seeker an opportunity to verify or alter the companion's perceptions in accordance with his awareness and experience. The reverse is also true. As the seeker reviews his experience, the companion has the opportunity to add other affirmative reflections that the seeker may have overlooked. The relationship ends with mutual understanding and appreciation. There are no secrets about what has been important for the seeker and what the companion has heard and affirmed. Openness and understanding at the time of termination allow for a smooth transition from the work of the spiritual companionship to the ongoing spiritual journey of each partner.

A third effect is interrelated with those already mentioned. Healthy closure provides a format for both partners to let go of the spiritual relationship and to live on in forming new spiritual partners—formal or informal. There are a sense of fulfillment and a recognition that what has been gained through the relationship is now an inner resource for the life of the seeker. The seeker is affirmed in his growth and is able, while appreciating the relationship, to let go of needing it at this time. The companion is affirmed and gains insights into her ability to be with the seeker on his spiritual journey.

Both partners recognize that spiritual growth has no ending in human time and space. Termination of the spiritual companion relationship does not say, "I am finished with spiritual growth." In fact, the relationship may have enabled the seeker to desire more in-depth spiritual guidance through retreats or through a relationship with a differently trained spiritual guide. Whether the seeker plans to continue in a spiritual relationship of some kind or not, it is imperative that both he and the companion are able to let go of their relationship. The companion gains in self-understanding as a spiritual guide as she engages in new and different covenanted relationships.

A fourth effect is in the power of the process of termination. Many persons from our culture of disposable products and transient living have never experienced the reverence and comfort given to each partner when attention is paid to termination issues. Some have the lingering wounds of isolation, separation, and unresolved loss because people (or they themselves) have come and gone as if human relationships were disposable products. The companion's attentiveness to the process of termination teaches the seeker a new way of going about healthy leave-taking of a relationship that does not wound the spirits of persons involved.

It could well be that at the end of the covenanted period of the spiritual companion relationship, the seeker desires to remain in the relationship. This desire may surface as he and the companion are into the process of termination. In fact, it is a good habit not to continue beyond the initial covenanted period without reviewing the past and setting a new covenant for a second period of time.

Both the seeker and the companion must reflect on their openness to continue. A healthy emotional check-in at this time is to ask oneself, "Am I free to terminate this relationship?" Unless one is free to let go of the relationship (at any time), one is not free to make a covenant to remain in the relationship. To be free to say yes to a commitment of companioning, a companion must be free emotionally to say no to such a commitment.

The Process

When the companion relationship comes to an end, both partners experience the loss and are in need of expressing their response to the loss. The expressions of loss embody feelings associated with the meaning of the relationship for both partners. These expressions also include aspects that were disappointing or are yet incomplete.

As in any phase of adaptation to a loss, the spiritual companion partners process how they will relate differently with each other after termination. The relationship is terminated, yet both partners have been affected and do not dismiss each other as if the relationship never happened. Both lives are different because of the relationship. The companion may wish to continue to pray for the seeker, for example. Many find it helpful to include a certain ritual that marks the end of the companion relationship. This ritual is in addition to (or is included with) the verbalization rituals of affirmation, meaning, disappointment, and promise of future relating.

The companion's astuteness will allow her the proper pace and timing to introduce the process of termination. Her active listening and attentiveness will also enable her to follow the lead of the seeker who may introduce some of the elements at their session. The companion is to keep two points clearly in mind, however, in her initiation of the process.

First, she must be aware not to initiate the process too early. For example, three sessions before the end, the seeker (or the companion) may feel the anticipation (anticipatory grief) of the end time and move into termination before the covenanted period is complete. If the seeker initiates this, the companion hears him as one in anticipation and responds accordingly. The seeker may state, three sessions in advance, "In thinking about our time together I can see how . . ." The companion, avoiding entering into premature termination, may respond, "It sounds as if our time together has been helpful to you. I am grateful for that for you. Yet I wonder if you are feeling some anticipation of our relationship ending?" or "I hear your celebration of what this has meant to you. Would you be able to say more about what prompted this review at this time?"

Second, the companion in initiating the process does not demand that the seeker enter into all its aspects. It is her responsibility to reflect on the seeker's journey, to offer feedback on the meaning of the relationship, and to let the seeker know how she will continue to remember him in the future. Her participation leaves room for the seeker to respond accordingly, yet he may not wish to respond in like manner. She encourages and assists him yet leaves the choice to him. For example, as she shares the meaning of the relationship to her, she pauses, allowing the seeker to absorb what she has said and to respond in any way that he wishes. If, after a brief period, the seeker does not respond, the companion may inquire if what she has said coincides with his experience.

In summary, termination of the spiritual companion relationship includes the following steps.

1. At the end of the second to last session, the companion should state that the next session is the last one and suggest that the seeker might want to reflect on his journey over the period of time of the relationship. She promises to do the same and to share her reflections in the next session.

2. The companion and the seeker agree that some time will be spent during the last session in review and reflection together.

3. The companion suggests that the seeker may want to consider a ritual that would be important for him to end the next session and the relationship. She makes it clear this is not necessary; it is only a suggestion.

4. The last session begins like any other with prayer or whatever the usual beginning has been.

5. The companion waits for the seeker to begin with his agenda. If he begins as planned, the companion follows his lead. If he begins with some new information or concerns, the companion may respond by affirming that she has heard him and then ask, "Since we agreed last time to spend some time this session on closure, do you want to explore (mention new topic) for ten minutes and then reflect on how our relationship has been for you, or is there a connection between (mention it) and your feelings about our relationship ending?" She follows the lead of the seeker while reinforcing that spending some time in closure is important.

6. The companion and the seeker share their reflections of their time together. The companion's reflections are in relation to the seeker. The companion may begin by saying, "Over the last months, I have experienced you as (give an image) . . ." Or the companion may say, "I want to affirm your consistency and sincerity on your spiritual journey. You have (name what has been heard in the past) . . ." The companion pauses for the seeker to respond if the companion has spoken first. If the seeker begins, the companion follows the lead by affirming and adding her positive reflections.

7. The companion shares what the relationship has meant to her. For example, "I have felt honored to be with you these months. Thank you for caring enough about yourself and our relationship to trust me." Or she may say, "I have been deeply moved by your commitment to living a Christian life. Your journey has been a help to me. Thank you." Or she may share, "I have come to know the power of God's love in working where 'two or three are gathered together.' Our times together have been holy times for me. Thanks." The companion pauses and allows the seeker to respond. She acknowledges any feedback received from the seeker. Affirmations must be

recognized and received for the seeker to maintain a sense of power in the relationship.

8. The companion then might request, "Is there anything that you feel disappointed about or wish would have been different during our times?" She acknowledges them and asks clarification if she does not understand the seeker's response. This is not a time for argument. This is a time for feedback and sharing. The companion may wish to offer some disappointments relative to herself. For example, "I am sorry I had to cancel two of our appointments because of illness." The companion's disappointment that the seeker was not more this or that, or did not take her guidance as she wanted, is not to be shared here. This disappointment has more to do with the companion than with the relationship; the companion's supervisory or consultative relationship is the arena for her to explore these kinds of feelings.

9. The companion promises to remember the seeker: "I will continue to pray for you," or "If I can be of help in the future, please feel free to call. If I am not able to help, I will let you know." She pauses to hear if the seeker wishes to offer a promise or commitment of prayer for her from this time forward.

10. The companion and the seeker ritualize the end: "How might we go about ritualizing the end of our time together?" Often, a psalm reading, a reflection on a prayer the seeker wrote, and a spontaneous gathering prayer of all that has just been reviewed are helpful rituals. Sometimes a handshake or other form of typical leave-taking is what the seeker is most comfortable with, and additional ritualizing is not necessary. Going out to dinner or lunch afterward may also be appropriate if the seeker suggests it.

Questions for Reflection

1. Recall a time when you were involved in the termination of a relationship. What was helpful and what was unhelpful about the way it was terminated?

2. What elements of termination reviewed in this chapter are new to you? What is your reflection on using these elements?

3. Do you have a natural style in ending relationships? Do you walk away? Do you leave and then emotionally return time and time again? Do you tend to bring closure in some way?

4. How will your natural style affect how you facilitate the termination of a companion relationship?

Reflect on Matthew 26:26–30 or Luke 22:14–20. What elements did Jesus include in his leave-taking? Reflect on Deuteronomy 34:1, 4–9 or John 3:20–30 in light of the elements necessary for terminating a companion relationship. Pay attention to what you discover. Pray the following litany (or write your own) as you complete the journey of this book:

I (We) give you praise, God of my (our) journey,
—for the power of love, the blessing of friendship, the mystery among us.
—for the wonder of growth, the kindling of trust, the taste of transformation.
—for the miracle of life, the gift of becoming, the grace of companionship.
I (We) give you thanks, God of my (our) journey,
—for strength, support, energy, and love from others.
—for the desire to continue on, to be a spiritual companion for others.
—for belief in vulnerability and strength.
I (We) ask forgiveness, God of my (our) journey,
—for times I (we) held on too tightly.
—for saying no instead of yes at times.
—for not listening to you or others at times.
I (We) ask your blessing, God of my (our) journey,
—to live life as humanly as I can.
—to be open, vulnerable, and a faithful steward.
—to never forget why I am who I am, loved by you.

Different Prayer Forms

This appendix serves as a review of prayer forms already mentioned or suggested at the end of a chapter and an explanation of the methods of other prayer forms.

Journaling

Journaling focuses on one's interior movements and often becomes a record of one's spiritual journey. Journal writing aids one in discovering who one is, one's deepest longings, and how God is present with him. The exercise at the end of chapter 2 gives the methodology for journaling; the exercise at the end of chapter 3 gives the method for reflection through the use of dialogue. Journal writing can be an excellent resource for the seeker to share his prayer experiences with the companion. Writing a letter to God, Jesus, or another and/or writing a letter to oneself from God, Jesus, or another (in response to one's letter or as the initiator of this type of correspondence) are also forms of journaling prayer. The suggested exercise at the end of chapter 4 is such a prayer.

Centering

Centering is often without words, although a means to enter into it is the use of a mantra, which is the repetition of a single word or phrase. Centering opens oneself to the Spirit dwelling within the person. It is a point of stillness within, where one experiences being absorbed by God's life-giving presence. The exercise at the end of chapter 5 invites the companion/reader to center prayer on various images of God. Under "Questions for Reflection" at the end of chapter 3, question 6 invites the reader to enter into this form of prayer using a mantra. Centering prayer can be done individually or in the company of others.

Active Imagination

Active imagination, as discussed in chapter 4, draws one into a particular scene of scripture or into the words of an icon or nature. In activating the imagination, a person uses one's senses to contemplate and to be present with the Divine. Using the imagination helps one become consciously aware of one's deeper realities, meanings, and life-giving energies that are present yet hidden in the innermost levels of one's being. Use of images is very important in one's holistic growth and, when done in the context of prayer, can be a powerful source of spiritual transformation.

If a group is involved in using images, the scriptural passage is read aloud for all to hear at least two times with three- to five-minute intervals between the readings. After the second reading, the group members share briefly what they have heard, felt, experienced. All members listen. There is no discussion. The reading is read a third time, after which there is a quiet period of at least five minutes. Members share the messages they heard and what they identify as their responses. In contemplating a scriptural passage, the individual enters into the story as if one were there.

Here are the steps:

1. Watch what happens; listen to what is being said. What is the context, and where is the story taking place? Is it familiar to you? Become part of the scene by assuming the role of one of the characters or by placing yourself in the scene—is it natural or unnatural for you to be there?

2. Ask, What difference does being there make for your life, your family, your society if you take what you hear seriously?

3. Be with Jesus or God.

4. Ask, What does Jesus or God say to you directly?

5. Respond to what you hear or feel. You may wish to write your response in a journal. (At the end of chapter 5 the reader was invited to enter into the prayer of active imagination with Luke 8:16–18.)

Guided Imagery

Guided imagery is a form of meditation that is similar to Jesus' use of parables and stories. As in active imagination, this prayer form uses the power of the imagination to release into consciousness what is lying dormant in one's inner self. In this prayer form there is an external guide who leads the person(s) into a scene. The guide leads one into a space wherein the person feels free and comfortable. This form of prayer can be used as an affirmation of one's core goodness, as a way of listening to the word of God in one's own life, in nature. Use of scripture or other scene is appropriate.

Here are two examples of guided imagery. The first uses the story of Luke 9:10–17, the feeding the five thousand. The second is nonscriptural. A seeker may wish to tape-record such a guided imagery and use it repeatedly for his prayer. Hearing one's own guidance can be powerful. Sharing one's experience with the companion guide and group is very important. Initially, one may need to write down his experiences before choosing what to verbalize with others. Some time should be given for this exercise.

EXAMPLE 1

Instructions by leader (instructions and images are said slowly with sufficient time for people to respond): Place yourself in a comfortable position. Allow yourself to relax. If you can, close your eyes. Imagine all the tension of the day draining out of your body through your toes. Try to let go of anything you are worried about. Set it aside. You can pick it up later if you wish to. Now, pay attention to your breathing, exhaling, inhaling. Relax.

Now imagine yourself in Bethsaida. You, Jesus, and the other disciples have come here for privacy and quiet, yet you are in the midst of thousands of people. You have labored all day among the people. Jesus, you notice, is exhausted from welcoming the people and performing miracles.

You pause to think about all that is happening. You feel good about your day's labor with Jesus. Yet you and the other disciples are concerned—you are tired, Jesus is tired, the people have no food or place of shelter. What particular feeling do you have? What do you want to happen?

You approach Jesus and say, "Send the crowd away, so that they may go into the surrounding villages and countryside, to lodge and get provisions; for we are here in a deserted place." You feel strong in advocating for the people.

But Jesus looks at you and says, "You give them something to eat."

How are you feeling now? What thoughts do you have? You find your voice again and remind Jesus that you have only five loaves and two fish. Did he want you to buy some more? You are a little perplexed. You wait.

What are you feeling? How do you feel toward Jesus? Then, Jesus tells you to have everyone sit down in groups of fifty. You follow Jesus' instructions.

Now, you go back and get the baskets containing your meager five loaves and two fish. You bring them to Jesus who raises his eyes upward, blesses them, and breaks them. You watch in wonder.

What are you feeling? What are your desires? What do you think of Jesus at this time?

Now, you hear Jesus telling you to distribute the food. You begin to do so. As you distribute you realize that the food is not running out. Everyone is eating; no one is left out.

You stop amidst the crowd. You look at Jesus. You look at the crowd. As you take in the scene you remember that just a few minutes ago Jesus told you to feed the people. You had no way of doing that with the provisions you had.

What have you learned from this event? What will you tell your family when you next visit them? Now, spend a few minutes in quiet prayer, and when you are ready, open your eyes and come back to this room.

EXAMPLE 2

Place yourself in a comfortable position. Allow yourself to relax. If you can, close your eyes. Imagine all the tension of the day draining out of your body through your toes. Try to let go of anything you are worried about. Set it aside. You can pick it up later if you wish to. Now, pay attention to your breathing, exhaling, inhaling. Relax.

Now, take yourself to your favorite spot—a place you have been to or a place you would like to go. Look around you. If you are outside, are there trees, sand, people, animals? What color is the sky?

Or are you indoors? Where are you? In a room? What room? Is it in a house? A school? A library? What color are the walls? Is there any furniture? Is anybody else around?

Now, feel the air around you. Is it warm? Cold? Clear? Foggy? As you finish exploring your surroundings, you sense a real peace and safety in this spot, your spot, your favorite spot. You walk around a bit.

Finally, you stop. Your whole body feels free, safe, and at peace. You turn to your side, and as you do so, you notice someone is there—you sense that person has been there the entire time.

You feel the love and life being sent to you by the other. Somehow you know the love and life are just for you. Do you know this person? How do you feel?

After a pause, the other asks if there is a gift you would like. You think about it. Is there something you need? How do you feel about asking for what you need? Are you willing to receive it? Are you trying to argue against it? Are you afraid of it? Do you need to say anything before you ask for what you need?

You say it. You wait. The other waits. Finally, in this safe and comfortable place of love and life, you ask for something. It seems that no sooner do you ask than you receive it. It is yours.

What feeling do you have? Did you thank the person? What are you thinking? Does having this gift from this person change who you are? Will you be different? Notice yourself and your feelings about yourself. Is there anything you want to tell the other person about the meaning of the gift for your life? If so, do so.

When you feel that you are ready to leave your favorite place and return with your gift, open your eyes and come back to this room.

Use of Poetry, Art, Clay, and Music

Using poetry, art, clay, and music in prayer activates one's creativity and uses one's body as expressions of the inner life. A structured form of poetry writing was exemplified in the haiku exercise at the end of chapter 6. Writing a poem, drawing a picture or sketch, molding clay (children's or professional), and singing or listening to music are ways to express one's feelings and to describe one's experiences that cannot be expressed or described in verbal articulation.

The media of poetry, art, clay, and music also employ "putting oneself" in the expression of the senses of touch, sight, and intuition. This form of prayer may be used as an expression of the meaning of a scriptural passage as well. After reading and reflecting silently upon a passage, the individual expresses the fruits of his reflection through one of these media. If this is done in a group setting, the members may wish to share their artistic "products" with one another. If one is alone, the person may wish to record in a spiritual journal any discoveries made through this prayer form.

Use of Dance

Dance as a prayer form reverences one's physicality as an embodied person. God speaks through and in one's bodied self. Chapter 11 offers an exercise in becoming aware of the sacredness of one's body and being open to the word of God in response. Dance movement as a prayer form uses the body as the medium of expression. Walking or other physical activity that is a focused expression also serves as a form of prayer through the use of the body. Dance prayer is not an artistic rendition but an expression of oneself, of the self created in God's image. Here is a way of dance expression:

1. Give yourself plenty of room to move.

2. Warm up by following the toe-to-head body exploration given at the end of chapter 11. If you are doing this as a group, you may want to take turns leading movements of different parts of the body.

3. After warming up, become quiet and take several deep breaths, concentrate on inhales-exhales, hold your hand on your stomach, and feel it move as your stomach expands on inhales and contracts on exhales.

4. Begin to reflect on what life situation is foremost for you and what feelings this situation brings up for you. If you are in a group setting, share these reflections with a partner.

5. You and your partner may wish to identify a scriptural passage that speaks to your situation. If so, notice with whom or what you identify at this time. Where in your body do you respond? Or you may want to identify where in your body you respond to or feel the feelings your situation brings up (e.g., your neck, your shoulders, your sinus cavity, your urinary tract, your knee).

6. With music as a background, spend ten to twenty minutes moving the feelings that you have. Get your whole body involved; exaggerate each movement—twisting in pain, reaching out in need, walking tall with confidence and power, jumping with joy. You must move—no sitting or standing still.

Do not be so intent on the precision of your movement as much as on the quality of expressing the feeling. When doing this as a group, the key element is not miming others or even watching others.

7. When you are finished with your expression time, allow yourself quiet as a way of gathering in the experience. What feelings do you now have? What discoveries did you make? In a group you may want to share your dances and their message for you. If you have done this alone, write about it in your journal.

Examen of Consciousness

Examen of consciousness is an exploration of how God is present within the events, circumstances, feelings of one's daily life. It is particularly helpful as a daily practice for persons desirous of a deeper awareness of and commitment to their response to God's daily love and action in their lives. As in any structured prayer, the examen is not to be a duty but a chosen form of prayer by the seeker. An exercise at the end of chapter 9 gives the method of examen.

Focusing

Focusing as a prayer form taps into one's "bodily knowing." This prayer can be done singly or in a group and is to be facilitated by another person. Focusing is generally not for everyone and is probably most effective when the level of trust is well established between the seeker and the companion.[1]

1. Sit in a comfortable position with your feet flat on the floor and your hands in an open position. (Suggestion: the facilitator verbally affirms the presence of God and seeks grace for this time of reflection.)

2. Close your eyes and allow yourself to go within yourself. Being aware of yourself, focus on your inner being. (Pause.) Is anything there disturbing you or disrupting your calm and inner emptiness? Is there anything keeping you from feeling good?

3. When you are ready, would you let me know by nodding your head or by responding verbally, indicating yes or no. (Facilitator waits for response— from every member if in a group.)

4. Imagine placing what is keeping you from feeling good at your feet or throwing it over your shoulder for now. Let me know when you are ready to go on. Indicate by nodding or by verbally responding with "okay." (Pause. Wait for responses.)

5. If you set something outside yourself, spend a few moments and experience how your body feels now. (Pause.)

6. Is there anything else that is keeping you from feeling good? If so, please let me know by nodding or by responding verbally with a yes or no. (Wait for responses. If "yes," repeat process above.)

7. Allow yourself a few moments to discover things—not problems—that are important to you (e.g., a dream, a challenge, something you are excited about). As you identify these, place them outside yourself as well. When you are ready to go on, please let me know by nodding or by responding verbally with yes. (Pause. Wait for responses.)

8. When you are ready, return to what you have set aside. Ask yourself if any of these feels as a top priority—has the most energy, the greatest hurt, feels the heaviest or lightest. Ask your body if it is okay to spend some time with this. If your body is willing, bring your top priority back into your body. Let me know when your body has received this. (Pause. Wait for responses.)

9. What is your bodily experience? How does this thing feel in your body now? Where do you feel it? Try to be with this thing with your whole self. Can you hold it in your body, being gentle, caring, and nurturing? Can you hug it, put your hand on it, set it next to you? What is the best way for you to carry it in your body? (Pause.)

10. Now, stay with how this thing feels in your body. Notice if anything comes—an image, a word, a phrase—that fits your experience. (Pause. When you are ready to go on, let me know.)

11. As you begin to end this period of reflection, become aware of any movement that took place for you. Recall how it felt in your body. (Pause.) Recall images or words that surfaced. (Pause.) Now attend to how you feel inside at this time. (Pause.) Savor this place where you are stopping. (Pause.) Reverence and celebrate your holy place. (Pause.)

12. When you are ready, come back to this room.

The seeker may wish to write his discoveries in his journal or share them verbally at once. Group members should be given the same option. The companion/facilitator may then ask, "What might God be asking of you at this time?" or "Is there a word from God for you today?" The group time of focusing is brought to a close with a brief period of quiet reflection after which the facilitator responds with "Amen."

Use of Dreams

Dreams are powerful messages that help people bring to conscious awareness what they already know unconsciously. Symbols, images, and messages in dreams are important factors to attend as part of the spiritual life. The meaning of one's dream always rests with the dreamer. The event(s), circumstances, and encounters in dreams are experiences (generated by the subconscious or unconscious) that the seeker has had. Dreams reveal the deepest part of oneself. Thus, dreams are "material" for discovering the Divine in one's life.

The spiritual companion can assist the seeker in finding meaning by suggesting connections from the Christian tradition or from other sources. For example, water is symbolic of cleansing, of baptism, of new life, of refreshment. Or a desert represents barrenness, dryness, thirst, heat. Or a large building may represent something mighty, oppressive, powerful, protective. The companion can also assist by asking the seeker to reflect on his feelings during the dream and immediately upon awakening: "What might these feelings be telling you?"

As the seeker shares his dream(s), the companion listens for connections yet does not offer her suggestions until the seeker has had a chance to say what it means to him. As dreams are explored, the companion responds as she would in being with the seeker in exploring any other experience. The seeker who is going to share dreams would be advised to keep a dream log or journal to track themes.

Appendix B

Learning as a Community

L earning the art of spiritual companionship is best achieved through the practice of this ministry and the reflection with others on how one utilized the skills and on oneself as a practitioner. Learning happens within the context of the community in which peers share their experiences, insights, and learnings, and reflect together for mutual growth and development.

The method of practice and reflection on one's experience provides the framework for those responding to the call of spiritual companionship to integrate the knowledge about the relevant concepts and issues with personal formation and the being with another as spiritual companion. The communal nature of the learning environment parallels the ground of spiritual companionship as a ministry within a faith community among peers. Each person brings to the community his or her gifts of the Spirit that have been developed and enriched through a particular set of life experiences.

The contents of this book offer the material and the reflective questions to be incorporated in a faith-based community training program. This appendix outlines the components for a comprehensive community-based program to be offered through congregations, seminaries and religious formation groups, clergy groups, religious women and men, faith-sharing groups, base-Christian communities, and other community groups desirous of becoming more effective ministers of care as spiritual companions.

Specifically, this appendix answers the questions "How is a program set up?" and "What is to be included in the training of spiritual companions?" The program outlined here is not a cookbook recipe but a guide for communities wishing to equip themselves for this ministry. Each group will want to adapt its program to fit its particular situation. It is, however, strongly recommended that the various components mentioned be included in the program to ensure quality and accountability of its trainees to the larger Christian community.

Time Period of Training

The program is for thirteen weeks or sessions for a time of three hours per session for the group as a whole. It is recommended that the first session be a full day in which the overall program is described, the group begins to form as a training group, members covenant to be peer-learners with one another, and periods of prayer and reflection on one's call to and understanding of the ministry of spiritual companionship are included. If less than three hours are available for each session, then the training period would be extended to allow sufficient overall time for each program component. The sessions may be weekly, biweekly, or monthly.

Selection of Participants

Some groups may be naturally formed for training because of their seminary affiliation (e.g., if done through a seminary colloquium), their religious group membership, or their faith-group partnership through which they enter into training. Other groups need to be formed. For example, if the training is offered as a program of a congregation, persons will need to apply and be accepted for the training. In selecting the trainees, sponsoring groups initiate an application process that includes some written information from the applicant, a face-to-face interview of the applicant with the program facilitator(s), and a reference for the applicant from another member of the congregation.

Written information need not be extensive but should include brief responses to (*a*) What leads you to want to be a spiritual companion? and (*b*) How have you experienced the call to this ministry? The sponsoring groups also may want to ask the applicant to write briefly about one's experiences of prayer, images of God, relationship with the Christian community, and one's experience of being companioned in the spiritual life. If these latter are not part of the written application, then they ought to be part of the interview process.

Prior to selection, the interviewing facilitators should be clear about the qualities of a person they are going to accept (refer to chap. 1). Even for groups already formed, it is a good practice for the facilitator(s) to interview the participants prior to the beginning of the program. The interview begins the relationship between member and facilitator(s) and is part of the training process in which participants must be willing and able to share their spiritual journey, to be vulnerable to receiving feedback, to offer honest feedback to others, and to be appropriately self-revelatory.

Facilitator or Group Leader

Each training group should have at least one facilitator or leader for every four or five persons involved. A facilitator should be a person with some knowledge of group dynamics and some experience in the supervision of others. A facilitator is a good listener and is able to foster group participation in giving feedback to one another and in self-revelation around the issues related to spiritual companioning. A facilitator should be a trustworthy person who has exemplified maturity in the spiritual life.

If the program with less than five persons has one facilitator, then that facilitator ought to be in a consultative or supervisory relationship with someone outside the program. If more than one facilitator is involved, then the facilitators should meet regularly for their own group supervision and consultation. The gifts of facilitation are enriched and fostered in one's relationship in community as the gifts of spiritual companionship are enhanced through the process of peer learning in community.

Opening Retreat

In the opening day of retreat the participants form as a learning community and begin the process of learning through prayer, input, observation, and feedback. The suggested format may include (*a*) a prayer ritual in which the members share what brought them to respond to becoming a spiritual companion (i.e., how do they perceive the call as a Christian?); (*b*) the sharing of personal stories, a sharing in which members tell, "What I would like you to know about me and my life's journey"; (*c*) an explanation of the format and components of the learning process; (*d*) one or two periods of input from the facilitator or an outside resource person addressing briefly the material of chapters 1 and 2 followed by discussion and reflective responses; (*e*) a role play (or actual situation) between the facilitators of a spiritual companion relationship with some follow-up explanation of basic skills used; and (*f*) a period of covenant making in which members share what they covenant with the group and what they need from the group.

In making a covenant one member may say, "I covenant to be open and to be faithful to coming. What I need from you is that you be honest with me." Another member may say, "I covenant to do my best. What I need from you is that you do your best." In the time of the role play, the forms for practicum feedback may also be introduced. Throughout the day, the community practice their listening skills with one another and become familiar with the process of sharing and reflecting together. Social times of meals and other space to become informally acquainted are interspersed throughout the day. The facilitator(s) or group leader(s) is engaged in the sharing and reflection as a peer with the other members.

Program Components

There are five major components of each session in the training program: the practice of spiritual companioning; peer practicum modules; teaching and discussion; group supervision; prayer and spiritual integration. Throughout the course of the training, each participant practices the art of spiritual companioning by meeting with a seeker on a regular basis.

The training companion and seeker covenant for the period of time of the training program. The seeker may be someone who has approached the companion trainee, a congregant who "volunteers," a person seeking spiritual companionship who is known by the sponsoring community or by the facilitator. It is not good for the trainee to companion a close friend.

The trainee makes it known to the seeker that she is in training and will maintain confidentiality throughout their time together. For the sake of those helping trainees, it may be well to review the meaning of confidentiality when one is supervised. To maintain confidentiality is a necessary way to respect the dignity of the seeker and to maintain the person's confidence in the companion. Therefore, speaking of what happened in a companion session in group supervision or seeking individual consultation around a particular concern is not breaking confidentiality. Speaking about what happened outside a supervisory or consultative relationship (individual or group) does break confidentiality because it shows disrespect for the seeker by inappropriately revealing his personal story. Insofar as it becomes known or intuited, the companion's inappropriate conversation weakens the confidence the seeker has placed in the companion. This breaking of confidentiality occurs whether the seeker knows or does not know that the companion has spoken about him to others.

After each session with the seeker, the companion trainee reflects on the session as part of her learning, spiritual growth, and preparation for group supervision. A reflection guide is used by the community members. The companion's responses may be written in a trainee journal that she is keeping or be recorded on the guide sheet. The companion trainee keeps these reflections throughout the program as a record of her own growth and development. In reflecting on the session, the companion trainee asks the following questions:

1. What emerged as the central issue(s) in the session? In other words, how was the movement of the Spirit in the life of the seeker and in my life being revealed?
2. What insights, perceptions, hunches, or feelings do I have about what is needed for the seeker's ongoing spiritual growth at this time?
3. What role did I play as a listening companion?
4. In what way was I satisfied or dissatisfied with my responses (internally and externally) to the seeker? What might be the underlying movement for me that contributed to these responses?
5. What do I need to understand or pursue more deeply in order to be a more effective companion with the seeker?
6. What learning did I derive from this session that will be important for me to remember?
7. What do I need to bring to the group for supervision as a responsible community member who is growing with others?

A second component is the peer practicum modules. The primary objective of the practicum is the trainees' development of the skills of effective listening as a spiritual companion (see chap. 3). The practicum also benefits the participants in enriching their listening skills, becoming self-revelatory, experiencing peer companionship, and being able to give/receive honest feedback and assistance as peer learners. Appendix C elaborates on this portion of the program. The time frame should be about forty-five minutes of the three-hour session.

A third component is teaching and discussion that draw on the materials in this book. A time of about one hour should be given to this component. A chapter a session would be assigned to the participants who would come to the next session ready to discuss the material. A facilitator would lead the discussion for the whole group. Group members and/or the facilitator may add additional insights or experiences on the topic. The reflection questions are part of the participant's "assignment" as well. After the discussion on the material, small groups of four or five (plus a facilitator) are formed, and the members share their responses to the reflection questions. This is not a time for argument. It is a time for listening to one another, seeking clarification from one another, and growing in understanding of and appreciation for one another. Through this time, the companion trainee is growing spiritually and is integrating the written material with her experiences and those of others.

Group supervision is a fourth component of the spiritual companion program. A period of about forty-five minutes should be allotted for this. The use of group supervision is detailed in Appendix D. Individual supervision is with the facilitator and takes place outside the group's scheduled time together.

Prayer and spiritual integration, the fifth component, are vital to the trainees' growth and development as a spiritual companion. In between sessions the community members are engaged in prayer and reflection based on their learnings in the session and on the reading material and prayer reflections at the end of each chapter. Members also engage in the prayer life of the larger Christian community in which they are members. In addition, each session is closed with a thirty-minute prayer/integration time.

If a particular prayer form has been suggested in the exercise at the end of the chapter being discussed, that may be used. If the chapter prayer form is not used, one of the additional prayer forms discussed in Appendix A may be used. Using these prayer forms facilitates the group prayer time and gives the participants an opportunity to experience different ways of praying. These, then, become integrated within the trainees' spiritual lives and are more readily incorporated in their practice of companioning.

Closing prayer may also take the form of the participants' sharing their prayer experiences, images, or insights gained in their spiritual journeys through the reflective exercises at the end of chapters or in their personal journal writing. This latter sharing begins with a period of quiet in which God's presence is recognized. Prayer in this way parallels the prayer that often takes place in the companion relationship as the seeker shares his experiences. All sessions are begun with a short prayer or period of quiet, recognizing that the Spirit is the teacher and trainer of the participants.

Termination

At the end of the training program the participants and facilitator(s) engage in the process of terminating their covenanted relationship with one another. This process includes the elements of termination mentioned in chapter 12. Sufficient time is given for this process. The last session can be totally devoted to the group's termination. At the end of the second to last session the group members agree to the process of termination. They also decide on what kind of termination ritual they want (snacks afterward, a social later, a prayer ritual and food) and who will be responsible for creating the agreed upon ritual. If there were more than one practicum module, the termination may be done in modules or as an entire training group. This decision can be made by the group. If done in modules, it is, however, a good practice to have a period for all group members to give some brief feedback to one another.

In preparation for the group termination process each member reflects on her growth and learning throughout the program and on her experience of the growth and learning of her peers. In such preparation, the companion reviews her reflections after each companion session, her responses to the reflection questions at the end of each chapter, her journal entries of prayer and supervisory times, her peer feedback to the practicum sessions, and her role engagement in the program. She will want to spend some time thinking about each of her peers and what she has learned from them and what she wishes to affirm in their growth and learning. She will also reflect on her hopes or needs for herself after the program and her hopes and future promises for each of her peers. These reflections will surface any unfinished business or any disappointments the trainee experiences.

During the last session each participant shares the fruits of her self-reflections and receives the reflective feedback about her from each of her peers. The evening is so scheduled that each member has an equal amount of time to give personal reflections and to hear from each member. One person at a time gives her self-reflections and receives feedback. The facilitators also engage in this process as they reflect on themselves and receive feedback from each member. The group may decide to allot some time to give feedback on the program and to offer suggestions for change. The evening is closed with the agreed upon ritual. The sponsoring body may wish to give each member a certificate of completion as a symbol of its recognition of the participant's ministry of spiritual companionship.

Appendix C

The Practicum Experience

The peer practicum module of the spiritual companion training program is done among four or five participants with a facilitator. If at all possible, the peer practicum group should remain constant throughout the training program; participants should remain in the same module and not switch from group to group. The participants form their own peer modules, although it is best to have both men and women and a diversity of cultures in each module if the composition of the training group permits it. Having the facilitator of the module as the individual supervisor of those in the peer group is also helpful.

The practicum modules are begun after chapter 3 is read and discussed. Generally, portions of this chapter are introduced through the role play/reflection time of the retreat. At least one entire session should be devoted to basic skills and an understanding of the pitfalls the members are to attend to in their practice of companioning. The chapter material is the beginning awareness and one's practice with a Christian seeker and with one's peers is the experience to be reflected upon in light of the knowledge gained.

In the practicum module group members rotate being a companion, a seeker, and the observers. Each week one member is a companion, another a seeker, and the other members are observers. The seeker comes prepared to share with the companion who practices her skills as a companion. The seeker and the companion enter into a spiritual companion relationship for about twenty minutes. The other members and facilitator observe the companion in her practice with the seeker.

This twenty-minute period is not a role play because the seeker shares something that is real and of concern or delight for him. The peer companion follows the agenda of the peer seeker for this period of time. Because these peers have some history together as members of the learning community, their knowledge of each other is considered "data" that had been shared in previous companion sessions. The practicum is to be considered an extension of the relationship of these peers and not a first encounter except early in the program.

Information known about the seeker outside the training program is not to be used by the companion during the practicum. For the companion to use such information without the permission of the seeker is a violation of the seeker's right of privacy and confidentiality because observers are present. If the seeker thinks certain past information is relevant to his agenda, he is responsible for bringing it up. The companion can ask (as she would in any spiritual companion setting), "Is there anything that you feel comfortable sharing that seems an important connection for you?"

During the twenty-minute session of companioning between the seeker and companion peers, the other members observe how the companion responds. The observers notice her body language and her use of the skills of listening. They are given an "Observer's Feedback" sheet on which they take notes and make comments. The facilitator also serves as an observer.

About fifteen minutes into the session the facilitator quietly announces that about five minutes are left. The companion then has the opportunity to practice her skills in bringing the session to an appropriate close. The session is not interrupted at any other time unless the facilitator observes that the conversation is becoming destructive to the seeker. This latter is rare, yet may on occasion occur.

At the conclusion of the twenty-minute period, there is a brief pause before feedback is given to the companion. After the pause, the companion is asked to give her reflections on her use of skills and on herself within the relationship. The seeker is then asked to reflect on his experience of the companion's ability to listen: Did he feel heard? Did the companion follow his lead? What was particularly helpful? What was not particularly helpful? Where did he think/feel the companion "missed" him?

The companion listens to the seeker's feedback and asks for any clarifications she may need in understanding the experience of the seeker. The observers then offer their feedback to the companion, beginning with the positive points and following with their suggestions for improvement in the companion's practice of effective listening.

The reflections of the companion and the seeker and the feedback of the peer observers should be specific. Here is one example: "When the seeker (use name) began, your use of reflective listening was very good. You mirrored what you heard when you said . . ." Here is another example: "You were most attentive to the seeker, yet I noticed you were not able to point out his inconsistencies when he said that he cared about his friend and also felt some bad feelings for this friend."

The companion listens to the feedback, seeking clarification when necessary. The facilitator's feedback is intermingled with those of the other observers. All feedback is focused on the companion and is not to be on the content of the seeker's agenda or on the seeker per se. If the seeker expressed deep emotions during the session, the facilitator and observers may inquire if the seeker is okay and is ready for the feedback session to begin.

At the conclusion of the feedback, the facilitator (and the observers as the group becomes more familiar with the process) asks the companion what she has heard and if there is anything she needs from her peers in processing this information at this time. The facilitator (or other observers) asks the companion what she knows about herself that helped her in her companioning and what blocked her in her being with the other. For example, what does she know about herself that helped her be empathic or prompted her to skip over the inconsistencies? The practicum is not a therapy session, yet is an arena for the trainee to reflect on herself and her needs based on this experience in developing as a spiritual companion. It allows the trainee to reflect on personal dynamics that inhibit her effectiveness as a spiritual companion.

At the end of the time period, the facilitator and observers give the companion their feedback sheets. Having the written words helps the peer companion review and further reflect on the feedback given to her. The companion may want to use this feedback as an agenda for her group supervision time. She may also wish to reflect and seek feedback on issues about herself that seem to block her effective listening.

It is common in the beginning sessions that the participants forget that they are persons with wisdom gained from their life experiences. While it is true that each one has a different kind of wisdom depending on age and experience, each has wisdom appropriate for who one is at this time. Thus, the facilitator may need to remind the members that they should tap in to their wisdom and spiritual resources in addition to what they are now learning in offering feedback.

A Sample Feedback Sheet

In giving feedback to your peer, remember to be specific and concrete. Also, do not expect that all elements of effective listening will be used. Attention/feedback is to be given in response to the following:

A. How does the companion begin the session? What skills were used?

B. How does the companion utilize skills throughout the session? Here is a review of the basic skills (highlight ones that your peer used in particular; comment on them and on those your peer may want to develop further):

1. *Presence*—here-and-now focus, bracketing, body language.
2. *Reflective Listening*—paraphrasing, mirroring, naming the unnamed, pauses.
3. *Empathic Responding*—vulnerable, able to enter the other's world, hearing feelings, boundary keeping, systemic awareness.
4. *Understanding*—ability to let go of personal ideas, concepts, lack of labeling, colluding, projection, stays with other's agenda.
5. *Confrontation*—deals with inconsistencies of feelings, words, ideas.

6. *Use of Self*—use of own feelings, thoughts, history for empathy and shares appropriately for sake of the other.

7. *Discernment*—assists in separating out priorities, in decision making.

C. How does the companion attend to the spiritual focus of the session? Is the person's relationship with the Divine considered? Should it have been?

D. How does the companion close the session?

E. Comments and suggestions for the companion (again, please be specific; use additional paper if necessary).

The Use of Group Supervision

"Supervision" is a word that often brings to mind the concept of one person being in authority over another. It is commonly associated with individuals' experiences of a "boss" or of someone who functions as a manager or a controller of others' functioning. It triggers for people the concept of a relationship in which one gets rewards or punishments. These concepts do not describe supervision in the art of spiritual companioning.

Supervision is part of the covenanted relationship of the members with one another. Like all the components of the program, it is the work of the Christian community that helps form "the saints for the work of ministry" (Eph. 4:12) of spiritual companionship. Supervision is the community's guidance with the peer companion on her journey of formation and development. In group supervision the members share their insights and gifts in caring for one another in such a way that each grows as a spiritual companion. In individual supervision, the facilitator shares her insights and gifts for the sake of the growth of the other. Supervision is an Emmaus walk among the members in which the supervisee asks the members to journey with her in uncovering and discovering new insights for her personal growth and development in the art of spiritual companioning.

The focus of supervision is the person receiving supervision; the context of the supervision is the trainee's practice of spiritual companionship. The peer presenting a situation or concern for supervision takes the leadership in getting her supervisory needs met. Group supervision is preferred over individual supervision as part of the learning community's peership.

Group supervision does not preclude, however, the trainee meeting with the facilitator for individual supervision when the need arises. Nor does it exclude individual supervision as an additional component if the facilitator is available and has some experience in the practice of individual supervision.

For group supervision to be effective, the participants must respect their own and others' experiences, insights, and value within the group. The participants must also be willing to be both assertive and open to change. The facilitator offers her input in group supervision, yet her primary tasks are to facilitate the participation of the group members, to maintain the focus of the supervision, and to offer support, affirmation, and clarification when needed.

Group supervision may be done in module groups or with the entire group, depending on the number of participants. The groups for supervision should be of such size as to allow each member a minimum of two sessions for supervision throughout the course of the program. Although the focus is on one peer, all group members gain insights that are helpful to them in their ministry practice. This same dynamic of group learning from a peer's presentation occurs in the practicum learning component. Effective group supervisions and practicums are beneficial for all participants who learn from one another.

The group may decide to rotate use of the group supervision, or at the time of supervision the facilitator asks who would like some time for supervision. The latter is generally preferred because it is difficult to schedule when a supervisory need may arise.

The trainee's reflections on a companioning session (see Appendix B) help her identify her agenda for group supervision. This agenda relates to places she felt stuck in the session, to her awareness of pitfalls in her listening, to her inner struggles in companioning, to her theological presuppositions that are being challenged, to changes in energy level she experienced in companioning, to concepts or issues the seeker raised that she struggles with, to her points of celebration. The supervisee may also wish to explore how her learning through the practicum time is being integrated in her practice of ministry.

At the beginning of the supervisory time, the companion states what she wishes the group to focus on for her growth. For example, "I need you to help me explore how to bracket my concerns when I am with my seeker." Then the supervisee gives a brief explanation of the context of the session in which she was unable to bracket her concerns. For example, "This is the third session with my seeker. We have been meeting every other week, so I have known this person for six weeks. Up until this session I felt connected and focused with the person. This time as he talked about his relationship with God I felt myself drifting off, and it was hard to stay with him. I don't know what happened."

At this point, the group members may need more information in order to respond to their peer's request for supervision. They may ask, "Could you tell us more about what the seeker was saying about his relationship when you began drifting?" This is a clarifying question for content of the session that may have initiated the drifting. Or the group may ask, "Could you say more about where you went when you drifted?" This is getting more information about the peer in the session. The supervisee and group continue to engage each other in exploring how the seeker's image affected her, how her drifting helped her, if there was anything that offended her, what feelings she had as she listened. A rule of thumb in supervision is the same as in spiritual companioning (i.e., the group is helping the individual bring to conscious awareness what is unconsciously already present within her). In this example, the group is helping her uncover and discover what is preventing her from bracketing her concerns when the seeker speaks about his relationship with God.

If the supervisee is unclear in her need for supervision, the facilitator and group members will want to help her clarify her need before going on. For example, a supervisee may begin, "I need help in being with my seeker." This is very general and can lead the group members to go off on tangents not helpful to the supervisee. They may need to inquire, "In what specific way do you need help?" If the person says, "I don't know," then the group may ask for a brief vignette of the companion session to help the supervisee clarify the specific focus of her need. Learning how to use supervision often involves learning how to identify one's needs from the community and to have confidence enough to ask for assistance. Although asking for supervision is the mark of a strong and competent person who knows personal limitations and the value of community consultation, persons can feel a tension between being competent and being needy.

Group supervision is not an interrogation or a collection of a lot of data by the group members. Rather, group supervision entails members listening to one another and dialoguing around the context the supervisee presents. Information may be needed for clarification as in the example above. Yet the exploration of supervision by the group is an engagement of the group in response to the supervisee. For example, if one group member asks what feelings the supervisee had in listening with her seeker (see above), another member ought not to immediately jump to a new topic or unrelated question. The members "play off" one another and interact with the supervisee. If the supervisee responds to the feeling question with, "I sort of blank out," then another member may ask, "Can you say more about blanking out?" Or someone may say, "If I were in that situation, I can imagine feeling angry. Could you have blanked out in order not to feel angry?" The skills of companioning are the skills of group supervision with a focus on the supervisee peer.

An individual may desire the group to reflect with him on points of his spiritual journey. For example, a supervisee may ask for some time because "I am really struggling with the image of God as Breath. I understand how God can be so imaged, yet I get stuck in allowing that image to be present for me." The supervisee would then share a little about when this is happening. His peers may want to know, "What images of God have been helpful?" or "What seems to be the importance for you to move beyond being stuck right now?" or "Could you say more about the meaning this image has for you?" Again, the group time is a time in which one's peers dialogue with the supervisee in helping him uncover or discover insights about his relationship with God and his desire to be open to God as Breath.

About seven minutes before the end of the group supervision time, the facilitator says there are seven minutes left and asks if there is anything more anyone wants to say at this time. The supervisee closes the session by reflecting to the group what she has gained from their input. Other members offer their gratitude to the supervisee for sharing and express what they learned from the supervisory session. As in the practicum all members are learning at the same time, even though the focus is on one member. Initially, the facilitator may be more involved in helping the group with this process of community relations; as the group matures as a learning community, the facilitator will be less involved in helping the movement of the process.

When there is more than one facilitator for the learning community, this same process of group supervision occurs among them on a regular basis. The facilitators become a peer community in addition to their larger peer relationship with the learning community. Their accountability to the community includes growth and development as facilitators. The focus of the facilitators' group supervision is the facilitator and her or his experience within the practicum and supervisory sessions and as a community member with other facilitators in being with the learning community.

Notes

1. The Art of Covenantal Partnership

1. Karl Rahner, *Foundations of Christian Faith: An Introduction to the Idea of Christianity* (New York: Crossroad, 1982), 120.

2. Group spiritual companionship is a relationship between a group and an individual companion who covenant to focus on the revelation of God in and through their experiences and function as a group. This type of group companionship can be very powerful.

For the sake of clarity in this text, individual companionship will be referred to rather than individual/group companionship. Concepts and references to the individual are applicable to groups as well. Also, for purposes of clarity, the companion or partner will be referred to in the feminine, and the one being companioned will be referred to in the masculine and identified as the seeker.

3. For more detailed description of Kohut's self-psychology, see Heinz Kohut, "Introspection, Empathy, and Psychoanalysis," *Journal of American Psychoanalytic Association* 7 (1960): 459–83. For specific application to spiritual companioning see C. Kevin Gillespie, S.J., "Listening for Grace: Self-Psychology and Spiritual Direction," in *Handbook of Spirituality for Ministers,* ed. Robert J. Wicks (New York: Paulist Press, 1995), 347–61.

4. Tilden Edwards, *Spiritual Friend: Reclaiming the Gift of Spiritual Direction* (New York: Paulist Press, 1981), 121.

5. Robert P. Maloney, "Listening as the Foundation for Spirituality," *Review for Religious* 51 (Sept.–Oct. 1992): 667. Parentheses are Barbara Sheehan's.

6. Francis Kelly Nemeck, OMI, and Marie Theresa Coombs, Hermit, *The Way of Spiritual Direction* (Collegeville, Minn.: Liturgical Press, 1985), 62.

7. W. A. Barry and W. J. Connolly, *The Practice of Spiritual Direction* (New York: Seabury, 1983), 47–48.

2. A Theology of Covenantal Partnership

1. Karl Rahner, "The Dignity and Freedom of Man," in *Theological Investigations,* vol. 2 (Baltimore: Helicon Press, 1963), 235–64.

2. Nemeck and Coombs, *The Way of Spiritual Direction,* 62.

3. The word "obey" comes from the root word *oboedire,* a contraction of *ob* and *audire* translated "to hear" or "to listen" in the scriptural sense as noted earlier.

4. Katherine Marie Dyckman, S.N.J.M., and L. Patrick Carroll, S.J., *Inviting the Mystic, Supporting the Prophet: An Introduction to Spiritual Direction* (New York: Paulist Press, 1981), 35.

5. Fran Ferder, *Words Made Flesh* (Notre Dame, Ind.: Ave Maria Press, 1986), 167.

6. See Roberto Assagioli, *Psychosynthesis* (New York: Penguin Books, 1980).

3. Effective Listening to the Companion and God

1. David W. Augsburger, *Pastoral Counseling across Cultures* (Philadelphia: Westminster Press, 1986), 27.

2. Thomas Moore, *Care of the Soul: A Guide for Cultivating Depth and Sacredness in Everyday Life* (New York: HarperCollins, 1992).

4. Prayer

1. Thomas Merton, *New Seeds of Contemplation* (New York: New Directions Books, 1961), 36–37.

5. Images of God

1. See the work of Dr. Carolyn Jacobs as discussed in Judette A. Gallares, *Images of Faith* (Maryknoll, N.Y.: Orbis Books, 1992), 204–6.

2. Kenneth R. Overberg, S.J., *Conscience in Conflict: How to Make Moral Choices* (Cincinnati: St. Anthony Messenger Press, 1991), 10–17.

3. Some scriptural references for images noted in this section are 1 Kings 5:12; Job 12:13; Ps. 104:24; Isa. 42:6; 2 Sam. 23:4; Ps. 27:1; Song of Sol. 1:5; Isa. 9:6; Pss. 78:39; 147:18; 104:3; Lev. 10:3; 11:44–45; 19:2; Exod. 15:3; Jer. 20:11; Jer. 50:29; Gen. 18:25.

4. See Luke 15:1–10; Matt. 18:10–14; John 17; John 14:6.

6. Personality Awareness

1. Augsburger, *Pastoral Counseling across Cultures,* 63.

2. Erik Erikson, *Identity and the Life Cycle* (New York: Norton, 1994).

3. Carol Gilligan, *In a Different Voice: Psychological Theory and Women's Development* (Cambridge: Harvard University Press, 1982).

4. Jean Baker Miller, *Toward a New Psychology of Women* (Boston: Beacon Press, 1976).

5. Gail Sheehy, *Passages* (New York: Bantam, 1984) and *New Passages: Mapping Your Life across Time* (New York: Random House, 1995).

6. Lawrence Kohlberg, *The Philosophy of Moral Development* (San Francisco: Harper & Row, 1981).

7. Mary Field Belenky, Blythe McVicker Clinchy, Nancy Rule Goldberger, and Jill Mattuck Tarule, *Women's Ways of Knowing: The Development of Self, Voice, and Mind* (New York: Basic Books, 1996).

8. Discussion of control and responsibility is based on the work of David Augsburger, *Pastoral Counseling across Cultures,* 97–102.

9. Carl G. Jung, *Psychological Types* (Princeton, N.J.: Princeton University Press, 1976), and Isabel Briggs Myers and Peter Briggs Myers, *Gifts Differing: Understanding Personality Types,* 3d ed. (Palo Alto, Calif.: Davies Black, 1995).

10. For more detailed information on each type see Richard Rohr and Andreas Ebert, *Discovering the Enneagram: An Ancient Tool for a New Spiritual Journey* (New York: Crossroad, 1990), or Don Richard Riso, *Personality Types: Using the Enneagram for Self-Discovery* (Boston: Houghton Mifflin, 1987).

11. Karen Horney, *Our Inner Conflicts* (New York: Norton, 1992) and *Neurosis and Human Growth* (New York: Norton, 1991).

7. Being Transformed in God by God

1. Carol Ochs, *Women and Spirituality* (Totowa, N.J.: Rowman & Allanheld, 1983).

2. Francis Kelly Nemeck, OMI, and Marie Theresa Coombs, Hermit, *The Spiritual Journey: Critical Thresholds and Stages of Adult Spiritual Genesis* (Collegeville, Minn.: Liturgical Press, 1987).

3. Henri J. M. Nouwen, *Reaching Out* (New York: Doubleday, 1975).

4. Earle C. Page. Copyright 1982 Center for Application of Psychological Type. Used with permission.

5. Dietrich Koller, "The Nine Faces of the Soul of Christ," in *Experiencing the Enneagram,* ed. Andreas Ebert and Marion Kustenmacher (New York: Crossroad, 1994), 111.

6. Barbara Metz, S.N.D. de N., and John Burchill, O.P., *The Enneagram and Prayer: Discovering Our True Selves before God* (Denville, N.J.: Dimension Books, 1987), 87–161.

7. The author is grateful for the many white males and females, black men and women, gays and lesbians who have helped raise her awareness and effectiveness as a companion by their trust and sharing.

8. William J. O'Malley, S.J., "The Grail Quest: Male Spirituality," *America,* May 9, 1992, 405.

9. Ibid.

10. See Jerry E. Hargrove Jr., "Telling Our Stories: Ministry to the African-American Spirit," in *Handbook of Spirituality for Ministers, ed. Robert J. Wicks* (New York: Paulist, 1995), 520–30. The author is also grateful to Dr. Homer Ashby of McCormick Theological Seminary, Chicago, Ill., for his unpublished lectures and insights on African American spirituality.

11. Ibid., 528.

12. bell hooks, *Black Looks: Race and Representation* (Boston: South End, 1992).

13. Teresa E. Snorton, "The Legacy of the African-American Matriarch: New Perspectives for Pastoral Care," in *Through the Eyes of Women,* ed. Jeanne Stevenson Moessner (Minneapolis: Fortress Press, 1996), 50–65.

14. Ibid., 54. Quoting Jacquelyn Grant from *White Women's Christ and Black Women's Jesus: Feminist Christology and Womanist Response* (Atlanta: Scholars Press, 1989), 205.

15. Ibid., 63.

16. Craig O'Neill and Kathleen Ritter, *Coming Out Within: Stages of Spiritual Awakening for Lesbians and Gay Men* (San Francisco: Harper, 1992), 208.

17. The author suggests reading and praying with Chris Glaser's book, *Coming Out for God: Prayers for Lesbians and Gay Men, Their Families, and Friends* (Louisville: Westminster/John Knox, 1991). The three sections of the book are Part I: Created in God's Image; Part II: Called as Community; Part III: Citizens of a Commonwealth. The author also suggests reading Chris Glaser's *Come Home! Reclaiming Spirituality and Community as Gay Men and Lesbians* (San Francisco: Harper & Row, 1990).

8. Guilt and Shame

1. Augsburger, *Pastoral Counseling across Cultures,* 115.

2. See chapter 2 in this book.

3. James M. Bowler, S.J., "Shame: A Primary Root of Resistance to Movement in Direction," *Presence* 3, no. 3 (September 1997): 27.

4. Young Gweon You, "Shame and Guilt Mechanisms in East Asian Culture," *Journal of Pastoral Care* 51, no. 1 (spring 1997): 60.

9. Sin and Forgiveness

1. See Walter Wink, *Engaging the Powers* (Minneapolis: Fortress Press, 1992), 69–77.

2. John Patton, *Is Human Forgiveness Possible?* (Nashville: Abingdon Press, 1985), 149.

3. Ibid., 62.

4. William B. Oglesby Jr., *Biblical Themes for Pastoral Care* (Nashville: Abingdon Press, 1989), 114–49.

5. Dennis Hamm, S.J., "Rummaging for God: Praying Backward through Your Day," *America,* May 14, 1994, 22–23.

11. Survivors of Abuse

1. The use of the words "victim," "survivor," and "victor" carries certain implications that affect not only the seeker but also the companion's attitude in listening with the seeker. "Victim" implies an emotional image of hopelessness and helplessness, an emotional reality for the child being abused. "Survivor" implies an image of one hanging on, a reality for those whose resilience and inner resourcefulness helped them to live into adulthood in the face of childhood abuse. "Victor" implies an image that the adult has found and thrives in a new life that integrates the abuse experiences that no longer control one's freedom and spirit; one has been triumphant. The author is indebted to Rev. Dr. Claude Marie Barbour for the freeing/healing image of victor.

2. The purpose of this chapter is to raise awareness and to identify spiritual growth issues for the adults who were abused as children; it is not to deal with the psychological or psychosexual issues. Yet the companion must be aware that there is no evidence that correlates sexual abuse with a homosexual orientation among men or women. Many survivors (heterosexual, gay, bisexual, lesbian, "asexual," undecided) are challenged with confused feelings about their sexuality and with "performance anxiety." The latter can lead to fear and avoidance of gays or lesbians, to sexual acting out, to homophobias. For more on this see Mike Lew, "Sexuality, Homophobia, and Shame," *Victims No Longer* (New York: Harper & Row, 1990), 54–64.

3. See chapter 7 in this book.

4. James Newton Poling, *The Abuse of Power: A Theological Problem* (Nashville: Abingdon Press, 1991), 168–73.

5. See chapters 7 and 9 in this book.

Appendix A

1. Adapted from Peter A. Campbell and Edwin M. McMahon, *Bio-Spirituality: Focusing as a Way to Grow* (Chicago: Loyola University Press, 1985).

Index

abuse, sexual. *See* sexual abuse

African Americans: cultural images of self and God, 57–58; personality development, 67; prayer, 12; spirituality, 84–86; and systems of church, 60

Africans: cultural images of self and God, 57–58; personality development, 67; prayer, 12

anger, 108

apophatic prayer, 47

art, as prayer form, 50, 147–48

Asian Americans: cultural images of self and God, 57–58; personality development, 67; prayer, 12

Asians: cultural images of self and God, 57–58; personality development, 67; saving face, 95–96

Assagioli, Roberto, 28

Augsburger, David, 66; on authority 69–71; on shame, 92

authority: cultural understanding of, 69–71; and God images, 56

Barry, William A., 16

Belenky, Mary, 68–69

bipolar self-development, 5–6; and spiritual growth, 6–7

Bonhoeffer, Dietrich, 15

boundaries, 37; and abuse, 94

Bowler, James, 92

Burchill, John, 81

centering prayer, 144

Christian community of care, vii, 4; companion training program for, 152–57

Christian Scriptures: covenanted relationship in, 22–27; divine judgment and grace in, 103–4; forgiveness and reconciliation in, 105–8; on guilt and shame, 98–99; praying with, 49–50, 144–45

clay, as prayer form, 50, 147–48

collusion, 39

companioning relationship, 6; context of, 9–10; covenant of, 6–9; focus of, 10–13; rooted in divine, 28–29

components of training, 154–57

confrontation, 40–41

Connolly, W. J., 16

consolation, 51

contemplative attitude, 16–17; of God, 19

Coombs, Marie, 77–78

counseling, 9–10

countertransference, 33

covenant, 6–9; God's, 21; and Jesus, 22–27; and spiritual companionship, 25–27; of trainee and seeker, 155

covenantal partnership, 5–6; theology of, 18–29

covenanted relationship, 20–27; and Hebrew Scriptures, 20–22; and Jesus, 22–27; termination of, 7–8, 157

cultural context: affecting guilt and shame, 92, 95–96; listening within, 16–17; personality development influenced by, 67; self- and God images based on, 57–58; under-standing authority, power, and control within, 69–71